LEADING
WITH
Vision

LARRY LASHWAY

CLEARINGHOUSE ON EDUCATIONAL MANAGEMENT
College of Education • University of Oregon
Eugene, Oregon

Library of Congress Cataloging-in-Publication Data

Lashway, Larry 19—
    Leading with vision / Larry Lashway
      p. cm.
    Includes bibliographical references.
    ISBN 0-86552-138-7
    1. Educational leadership—United States. 2. School management and
organization—United States.   I. Title.
    LB2806.L27 1997
    371.2'00973—dc21   97-27661
                                                  CIP

Design: LeeAnn August
Type: 12/13.5 Garamond
Printer: Thomson-Shore, Inc., Dexter, Michigan

Printed in the United States of America, 1997

ERIC Clearinghouse on Educational Management
    5207 University of Oregon
    Eugene, OR 97403-5207
    Telephone: (541) 346-5044 Fax: (541) 346-2334
    World Wide Web: http://darkwing.uoregon.edu/~ericcem
ERIC/CEM Accession Number: EA 028 448

This publication was prepared in part with funding from the Office of Educational Research and Improvement, U.S. Department of Education, under contract no. OERI-RR 93002006. The opinions expressed in this report do not necessarily reflect the positions or policies of the Department of Education. No federal funds were used in the printing of this publication.

The University of Oregon is an equal opportunity, affirmative action institution committed to cultural diversity.

MISSION OF ERIC
AND THE CLEARINGHOUSE

The Educational Resources Information Center (ERIC) is a national information system operated by the U.S. Department of Education. ERIC serves the educational community by disseminating research results and other resource information that can be used in developing more effective educational programs.

The ERIC Clearinghouse on Educational Management, one of several such units in the system, was established at the University of Oregon in 1966. The Clearinghouse and its companion units process research reports and journal articles for announcement in ERIC's index and abstract bulletins.

Research reports are announced in *Resources in Education* (*RIE*), available in many libraries and by subscription from the United States Government Printing Office, Washington, D.C. 20402-9371.

Most of the documents listed in *RIE* can be purchased through the ERIC Document Reproduction Service, operated by Cincinnati Bell Information Systems.

Journal articles are announced in *Current Index to Journals in Education. CIJE* is also available in many libraries and can be ordered from Oryx Press, 4041 North Central Avenue at Indian School, Suite 700, Phoenix, Arizona 85012. Semiannual cumulations can be ordered separately.

Besides processing documents and journal articles, the Clearinghouse prepares bibliographies, literature reviews, monographs, and other interpretive research studies on topics in its educational area.

CLEARINGHOUSE
NATIONAL ADVISORY BOARD

George Babigian, Executive Director, American Education Finance Association
Anne L. Bryant, Executive Director, National School Boards Association
Esther Coleman, Executive Director, American Association of School Personnel
    Administrators
Timothy J. Dyer, Executive Director, National Association of Secondary School
    Principals
Patrick Forsyth, Executive Director, University Council for Educational
    Administration
Paul Houston, Executive Director, American Association of School Administrators
Samuel G. Sava, Executive Director, National Association of Elementary School
    Principals
Gail T. Schneider, Vice-President, Division A, American Educational Research Association
Don I. Tharpe, Executive Director, Association of School Business Officials International
Brenda Welburn, Executive Director, National Association of State Boards of Education

ADMINISTRATIVE STAFF

Philip K. Piele, Professor and Director
Stuart C. Smith, Associate Director for Publications

. . . .

WEBSITE

L earn more about ERIC by visiting this Clearinghouse's site on the World Wide Web. You can read descriptions of our current and forthcoming publications, learn how to submit documents to ERIC, view the full text of recent *ERIC Digests*, find out how to search the ERIC database, and learn about special projects we are developing.

Through the ERIC/CEM web site, you can also be transported electronically to the sites of other clearinghouses in the ERIC system and to other education-related web sites.

http://darkwing.uoregon.edu/~ericcem

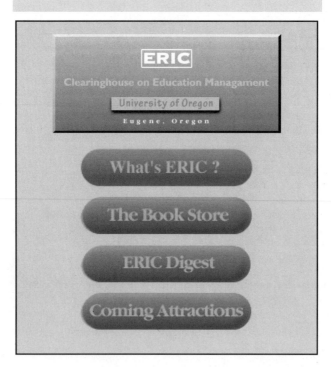

CONTENTS

ACKNOWLEDGEMENTS

Some of the material in this book originally appeared in a chapter I wrote for *School Leadership: Handbook for Excellence*, third edition (ERIC Clearinghouse on Educational Management 1997). I want to express my appreciation to Dr. Philip Piele and the Clearinghouse for offering me the opportunity to expand those ideas into this volume. I am also deeply indebted to Stuart Smith for his steady encouragement, judicious advice, and unfailing editorial support.

Additional thanks go to Dr. Linda DeClue at Bartholomew Consolidated School Corporation in Columbus, Indiana, for granting permission to reprint the district's vision statement (as well as for sharing her insights on the process), and to Mary Haynes, who allowed me to quote from her paper.

No work of this type would be possible without library support, and I've been blessed with an abundance of rich resources, including The Evergreen State College, Pacific Lutheran University, the Washington State Library, and Olympia Timberland Library. Their extensive holdings, helpful staff, and generous use policies made my task infinitely easier.

*L*arry Lashway is a writer and consultant who lives in Olympia, Washington. He is former director of the Teacher Leadership program at Silver Lake College, Manitowoc, Wisconsin. His previous writing for the Clearinghouse includes seven *ERIC Digests* and authorship or coauthorship of several chapters of *School Leadership: Handbook for Excellence,* third edition.

FOREWORD

The idea that organizations should have a sense of their direction is a relatively new concept. Most large organizations have been concerned historically with maintenance and stability, not with adaptation or direction. Organizational structure in the twentieth century has evolved with the goal of creating stability and predictability of function. Mission-focused, change-driven organizations have always been the exception.

All this has changed in the last two decades of the twentieth century. All organizations, public and private, are being challenged to focus on products or results. To do so requires a keen awareness of the environment surrounding the organization coupled with an internal cohesion that allows all the units and individuals within the organization to function in a concerted effort toward specified ends.

Educators particularly need what Larry Lashway offers in this book since schools are among the least able to adapt to this challenge. Their organizational structure emphasizes decision-making in isolation in an environment where the output measures are unclear, supervision is minimal, and links with the external world are often weak to nonexistent.

In such an organizational context, the most well-meaning of employees has to rely on his or her individual sense of right and wrong, and of organizational priorities. Compliance with those priorities is essentially voluntary; reward for compliance or accountability for noncompliance is minimal. How can change occur within such a structure? How can improvement be realized, quality increased, service improved, client needs better met?

The stakes of not addressing this challenge are increasing for educational leaders who are being held more accountable for systematic improvement of schooling. Administrators are expected to generate improvement in a system that is decentralized and where authority is diffuse. In spite of these constraints, there are administrators who have been and continue to be successful in bringing about change.

The research on effective schools over twenty years, for example, contains some consistent findings. One is the importance of a clear focus on academic learning by the school and a high acceptance of personal responsibility for student learning by teachers. Such schools see higher student achievement. But such schools do not necessarily have authoritarian administrative structures. How do administrators garner focus and concerted effort without resorting to dictates?

This book suggests one powerful tool: the creation of common agreement on and understanding of organizational purposes and direction, what has come to be known as an organizational vision. Lashway engages in an extended and comprehensive analysis of the concept of vision, an analysis that helps the reader understand the complexity of this term and the varying responses it evokes.

The term *vision* is deeply rooted in human culture and has many meanings, from clinical to mystical. For this reason it is an evocative concept, one that can inspire but also create anxiety. Some leaders emphasize the clinical dimension, the capability to design a rational planning process rooted in common understanding, while others seize upon the semispiritual dimensions of visions, those that promote a dedication and belief in the value and correctness of what one is doing.

Schools have struggled to strike a balance, to produce a blending of these differing aspects of vision, and to do so in ways that are consistent with the unique nature of schools as "captive" organizations, ones that cannot define any vision they wish but that are constrained by numerous forces. Lashway demonstrates how administrators have effectively used vision in a wide range of environments.

The process of vision-building was not commonplace in public education much before the late 1980s. Some schools had always possessed strong identities or cultures. But few, if any, had engaged in some systematic reflection or analysis of what they wished to become. Identity often arose from a founder or founders with a strong personal sense of what they wished education to be, or a particularly strong or long-lasting leader who consistently espoused an educational philosophy around which others could align. But these efforts defined the status quo; they did little to set a clear direction for the future, a path of improvement, a set of goals that could serve both to organize and inspire continued and future efforts. Often when the leader left, so did the vision.

Early efforts at vision-building were almost always associated with strategic-planning processes. The tenets of strategic planning, as applied to service organizations, emphasized starting by defining what the organization wished to become, then designing backward from that goal. The vision was the first step in the process. From this starting point, data on current functioning could be analyzed; goals, objectives, and action plans formulated; resources allocated; and efforts evaluated. Given the importance of the vision to the planning process, a great deal of time was often devoted to its creation.

The process of creating a vision required different constituencies, or *stakeholders* in the parlance of strategic planning, to communicate, to understand one another's points of view, aspirations, frustrations. Many of those who engaged in strategic planning described these aspects of vision-building as among the most valuable of the entire planning process. Unfortunately, when the vision was shared with those who had not participated in its creation, something was often lost in the translation. What had appeared so powerful to those who argued over its every word seemed somehow flat or hollow to those who read it from a dispassionate perspective. Vision statements blossomed in schools and administration buildings. But often little else followed or resulted.

The lesson learned is that vision is one dimension of a complex process of both organizational and cultural transformation. While it can be important as stimulus, catalyst, and compass, it needs a series of supports in place to achieve the goal of system improvement.

This book concludes by emphasizing the need to think about schools (and school systems) as learning organizations that continually encourage their members to perceive themselves as participants in a "learning community." This community becomes ever more adept at meeting client needs, addressing societal expectations, employing data effectively, and utilizing resources efficiently. Schools that can operate in such a fashion will be those that survive and prosper in the twenty-first century. Vision is one important tool to help schools adapt in ways that ensure their continued viability, legitimacy, and value as core institutions in our society.

We can be thankful that this book is much more than another survey of ground now familiar to many school leaders. Readers will be rewarded with an understanding of the visioning process that will help them manage its use in the educational improvement process. Moving from broad overview to very specific recommendations and models, Lashway enables the reader to learn in a few pages lessons that have taken others years to master. A great deal of experimentation has occurred, and this book elegantly captures the most important generalizations and conclusions regarding the effective use and limitations of the visioning process.

In this exceptionally well-written guide, administrators, teachers, parents, and community members will learn how to construct a vision that will energize their schools and inspire everyone to commit their energies to organizational excellence. I hope they will accept Lashway's invitation to harness the power that a vision for the future supplies for work in the present.

David T. Conley
Associate Professor
College of Education
University of Oregon
Eugene, Oregon

INTRODUCTION

My interest in educational vision began almost a decade ago as I was teaching a course on organizational change to a group of veteran teachers. One of the assignments asked them to design a school based on their own educational visions.

As the process unfolded, they reconnected with the ideals that had brought them into the profession, ideals they had pursued quietly but hesitated to discuss publicly. Experience had taught them that school reform was about politics, not education, and the best they hoped for was the occasional small victory within the confines of their own classrooms.

They found the assignment stimulating and sometimes moving but expressed doubt about its practicality. This was, after all, a classroom exercise; in the messy real world, there was a formidable gulf between stating a vision and actually implementing it.

I didn't have a satisfactory answer to these questions, and my own questions increased as I saw schools grappling with an unwieldy "vision process" in which committees of teachers, parents, and administrators labored to produce a formal statement that expressed their hopes for the future. The statements were often eloquent and soon adorned bulletin boards, newsletters, and annual reports. Yet, despite the utopian rhetoric that often surrounded the process, few schools seemed to be transformed by this exercise. Today, school leaders continue to use the language of vision when communicating with the public, but the underlying attitude often seems to be, "Been there, done that."

Just another passing fad? It may appear that way, but the organizational literature—in business as well as education—says otherwise. The consensus is clear: in today's turbulent environment, organizations cannot survive (much less prosper) without a well-focused vision for the future.

The problem is that the concept of vision has always been somewhat fuzzy around the edges. Sometimes it is described as the brainchild of brilliant thinkers, powered by intuitive, almost mystical glimpses into the future. At other times it is treated as the product of committees, methodically developed by patient, logical thinking. While proponents of vision tend to be evangelical in their enthusiasm, they are not always helpful in providing specific directions; the attractive rhetoric often seems disconnected from the everyday realities of running a school.

This volume is an attempt to clarify the issues surrounding vision by providing a basic conceptual framework. What is it? Why does it matter? How is it developed? In addition to discussing what researchers in education and business have learned about vision, I have also included some concrete exercises and activities for school leaders who wish to develop or renew the vision for their schools. These activities should be treated as starting points (or simply as food for thought), not as essential steps.

Like most Clearinghouse publications, this volume is a work of synthesis, designed to report on the existing literature rather than to create new theories. However, as with every synthesis, personal judgments and interpretations are inevitable. In the attempt to formulate a coherent picture from diverse sources, I may have seen implications or made connections that the original authors did not intend.

This is especially likely when the topic is vision, which is not backed by the kind of rigorous experimental studies that most people have in mind when they say, "Research shows...." The vision literature is an uneven mixture of enthusiastic advocacy, generic advice, and insightful analysis that does not easily lead to grand conclusions or simple formulas.

Thus, the material in this book does not confront school leaders with unequivocal demands to do things a certain way. Rather, it challenges leaders to think about purpose and possibility, and to ask, "Why are we here?" and "What should we do about it?"

Finally, I have a vision for this book: that it will provide school leaders with perspectives and knowledge that will help them fulfill their own visions. It's important for me to know if I've succeeded, so I invite you to let me know how this book did or didn't do the job. I can be reached by mail in care of the ERIC Clearinghouse on Educational Management, or via e-mail at llashway@aol.com.

ONE

THE VALUE OF VISION

As Emma Bronson addressed her classmates at Fredonia Normal School on a July evening in 1872, she reminded them that the diploma they were about to receive was a "holy trust" that would give them admission to "fields of labor wherein immortal minds are to be cultivated." Then, turning to her teachers, she said:

> If our hearts have been touched with a coal from your altar surely we shall perform the duties we are about to assume with becoming zeal. If we are as patient and faithful with our pupils as you have been with us, our efforts will be crowned with success. By example, as well as precept, you have taught that "Work is the weapon of honor, and he who lacks the weapon will never triumph." (*Fredonia Censor*)

Almost 125 years later, an aspiring teacher in Aberdeen, Washington, wrote:

> I want to be able to help children gain information, and gain it in a way that is fun, memorable and applicable to their lives. I want desperately to change the too often heard "I can't" into enthusiastic "I can."

Today's language is less ornate, but no less earnest. Across the gulf of 125 years and from opposite sides of the continent, Emma Bronson and Mary Haynes would recognize each other as kindred souls, driven by the desire to serve others and willing to work long hours to shape the next generation. Nor are they isolated examples; research continues to show that the overwhelming majority of teacher aspirants express a service ethic as their primary motivation for teaching (Robert Serow and colleagues).

So it's surprising to find that this individual idealism does not always translate into a collective sense of purpose. Ask teachers about the vision for their schools, and you're likely to get a puzzled look or a vague platitude like "meeting the needs of all students." Occasionally, they'll hand you a "vision statement" that some committee produced a couple years ago—if they can find it. Teachers often can speak eloquently about their personal vision, but it tends to remain private, something to be expressed within their own classroom, not paraded in the faculty room.

Admittedly, creating a clear, coherent institutional vision is not an easy task, especially for public institutions. Americans today seem increasingly divided over values, fragmented into dozens of competing interest groups. Whenever a school declares publicly, "We are going to move *this* way," a faction rises up to respond, "No, we ought to move *that* way." For wary administrators caught in the crossfire, it often seems easier to voice a few platitudes that smooth over these deep divisions, hoping they can quietly nudge the school in the right direction a little bit at a time.

Schools also seem caught up in what Joseph McDonald has called the "dailiness" of educational life: there are schedules to meet, curriculum to cover, and regulations to follow. Hundreds of unanticipated little problems bubble to the surface every day, demanding immediate attention. There scarcely seems time to reflect on visions of what could be—and even less time to engage in dialogue with those who have conflicting visions.

Even when schools do manage to formulate a clear sense of direction, they often have trouble moving beyond the initial aspiration, or they backslide after a few hopeful years. McDonald, drawing on his work with the Coalition of Essential Schools, says that genuine reform is achievable but "nearly impossible." Kenneth Tewel, who turned around a demoralized, ineffective high school in New York City, says, "Leading a school undergoing fundamental and comprehensive change is complicated, frenetic, almost always turbulent, and invariably messy." Visiting his former high school a few years later, Tewel found it had lapsed back into stagnation.

Despite these difficulties, schools today are under heavy pressure to find radically new directions. Critics routinely describe them as "nineteenth-century bureaucratic dinosaurs" that are "beyond repair" or "dysfunctional." Many educators, eyeing declining resources, expanded expectations, and a rapidly changing society, need little convincing.

Thus, school leaders in the 1990s find themselves enticed by the talk of visions for the twenty-first century but also skeptical and unsure of where to begin. Advice is plentiful but often vague; leaders are urged to "have vision" without being told what a good vision looks like or where it comes from.

Unfortunately, as David Conley and colleagues note, vision in school settings simply hasn't been studied much. We are only now beginning to see accounts of schools that have established a vision, and the results are far from consistent. Vision-building is still more of an art than an applied technical skill.

Yet it would be a mistake to consider vision a mystical process reserved for a few high-powered leaders. Increasingly, it is viewed as a core leadership task that must be mastered by *all* leaders—and one that can be. This chapter explores the basics: what vision is, what it accomplishes, and what role leaders must play.

THE NATURE OF VISION

Burt Nanus defines *vision* this way: "Quite simply, a vision is a realistic, credible, attractive future for your organization. It is your articulation of a destination toward which your organization should aim, a future that in important ways is better, more successful, or more desirable for your organization than is the present."

David Conley characterizes vision as an explicitly stated agreement on values, beliefs, purposes, and goals shared by a significant number of participants in an organizational unit. This agreement serves as a standard and reference point for making decisions.

James Kouzes and Barry Posner call vision a kind of "seeing"; that is, it creates images of what the future might hold. A principal interviewed by Linda Sheive and Marian Schoenheit exhibited this ability when he said:

> I believe you need to carry around dreams. You begin to see scenarios in your head. We're going to combine our two high schools some day, and I can already see the first assembly when all the kids come together. I can already see the parade through town when we celebrate it. When you're in a place long enough, you actually attend one of those scenarios [that you dreamed], that really is exciting.

Arthur Blumberg and William Greenfield identify vision with "moral imagination," a quality of character that gives someone "the ability to see that the world need not remain as it is—that it is possible for it to be otherwise, and to be better." In their view, vision is thus more than a technical task—it reflects the leader's values and is the source of his or her moral authority. Thomas Sergiovanni agrees, but emphasizes the collective nature of vision by calling it a "shared covenant."

THE CONTENT OF VISION

Discussing vision can be like eating cotton candy: tasty, but not much substance. Once you get past the glittering generalities, what's actually in a vision?

There's no single answer, since every vision reflects the values of a particular group of people in a particular school; a vision that energizes one school will fall flat in another. But we can make a few generalizations about the kinds of ideas that are found in visions.

1. *Visions are about what, and how, students will learn.* This is the foundation and the ultimate justification for any vision. Schools are here to serve children; a vision that ignores students is hardly worthy of the name. When principals, teachers, and parents take the time to reflect on learning, they might see any of the following possibilities:

- Students will spend less time memorizing and more time solving problems.

- Content will be presented holistically and thematically, not chopped into subject-sized fragments.

- The curriculum will aim at depth rather than trying to quickstep students through a budget tour of the encyclopedia.

- Learning will be a matter of collaboration and teamwork as much as competition.

2. *Visions are about social justice.* By committing themselves to educate virtually all children, American schools are an essential agent in maintaining an equitable society. To the extent that they distribute "intellectual capital" without regard for class, race, or gender, schools provide the foundation for a society that is democratic in spirit as well as law. Unfortunately, the practice has always fallen

behind the promise, so when some educators look at the future they envision other possibilities. Among them:

- Student opportunities for learning will be influenced more by students' interests and abilities than by class, race, or gender.

- Schools will respect and celebrate diversity, providing a model for an inclusive society.

- Students will develop a keen sense of social responsibility and a commitment to democratic processes.

3. *Visions are about the kind of professional environment the school will provide.* The quality of education for students is often related to the quality of working conditions for teachers. Too often, teachers have worked in an environment that offered little stimulation, support, and encouragement. Thus, the vision may include possibilities such as these:

- Teachers will work collaboratively to improve instruction, develop curriculum, and advance a common vision.

- Schools will become "learning organizations," providing intellectual stimulation and continual opportunities for professional development.

- Decisions will be made through dialogue and consensus rather than bureaucratic mandates.

4. *Visions are about the ways that schools will relate to the outside world.* As public institutions, schools have always claimed a special relationship with parents and community members. Yet they have often remained isolated from the social mainstream and frequently at odds with their constituents. Some educators can imagine different kinds of relationships:

- Educators and community members will find common ground through mutually respectful dialogue rather than political maneuvering.

- Schools will form external partnerships with businesses and community agencies.

- Student learning will expand beyond the classroom to include the entire community.

These are only examples, of course; the content of any vision will express the values and beliefs of those who nurture it. In fact, visions focus energy and reduce uncertainty by choosing one particular direction from a wide range of possibilities.

WHAT VISION IS NOT

Definitions of vision are still loose and unsettled, putting off some administrators who prefer projects with hard edges and measurable results. Some of the fuzziness is inevitable, since vision asks us to think about things that don't yet exist. However, we can improve our understanding by pointing out what *doesn't* constitute vision.

Vision is not feel-good rhetoric. Some schools, noting the uplifting images associated with visions, have treated the process as a public-relations exercise. Grandiose phrases like "recognize the unique needs of each child," "prepare for the technological challenges of the twenty-first century," and "develop responsible, caring citizens" make everyone feel good about schools, providing assurance that things are on the right track.

Elevated language can play a useful role, but vision is also a practical tool for planning, assessment, priority-setting, and time management. Kenneth Leithwood and colleagues (1994) say:

> Useful, defensible visions are the product of careful thought, systematic effort and continuous evaluation and refinement. They are not the fluffy products of armchair daydreaming which the term itself seems to suggest and many current administrators seem to believe.

Visions may seem to float above the fray, but they have little effect unless the leader takes them into the trenches.

Vision is not mission. Nanus asserts that mission is purpose, a statement of core principles; it answers the question "Why are we here?" Vision imagines how that mission will be fulfilled in the future.

Thus, a typical mission statement might look like this: "Asimov Elementary School exists to provide a positive environment in which all children can actualize their potential." For Nanus, this would not be a vision because it does not spell out a future state that is noticeably different from the present.

However, knowing the mission is essential for vision, since it points to the kinds of changes that are needed. If teachers at Asimov Elementary reach the conclusion that not all students are actualizing their potential, or that societal changes will make current methods inadequate, they must visualize a future in which the mission is fulfilled: "Asimov students will become skillful, self-directed learners by participating in a linguistically enriched, integrated curriculum, with portfolio-based assessment and a strong emphasis on self-evaluation." (However, another school with the same mission might arrive at a very different vision; as Kouzes and Posner note, each organization is unique, and there are many ways to achieve the same results.)

As a practical matter, the distinction between vision and mission may not be critical. Conley and colleagues note that many of the schools they studied seemed to use the terms interchangeably, apparently with no ill effect. As long as a vision includes both a strong sense of purpose and a picture of the future, it makes little difference what it is called.

Vision is not strategic planning. Another related term is "strategic planning," which has received considerable attention in the past decade. Like visions, strategic plans imagine a future state that is different; unlike visions, plans offer a systematic, sequential strategy for getting to the future. The entire plan is mapped out at the beginning with specific, quantifiable objectives, in enough detail that the entire process can be captured on flow charts (Roger Kaufman).

But the heavy emphasis on rationality and control makes strategic planning unsuited for the development of vision. Henry Mintzberg, discussing the impact of strategic planning in the business world, says, "Planning is fundamentally a conservative process: it acts to conserve the existing orientation of the organization, specifically its existing categories." Quoting Henry Kissinger, he calls planning "the projection of the familiar into the future."

Visions are goal-directed, but they don't always map out a clear pathway, especially if the goal is something that has never before been done. Some studies suggest that vision development is a looser, more improvisational approach than strategic planning. For example, Conley and colleagues found that in some schools the vision emerged only after several years of experimenting with alternative approaches. Apparently, teachers and administrators had to see some ideas in action before they were ready to articulate a vision they could commit to. Karen Seashore Louis and Matthew Miles found the same thing in urban high schools they studied.

In theory, the tools of strategic planning could be used for implementing visions. Kaufman, for example, portrays planning as a means of achieving a school's "ideal vision." However, the two approaches seem to have very different "flavors." Plans are roadmaps, offering a predictable itinerary; visions are more like compasses, pointing out the right direction, but leaving a lot to interpretation.

Vision is not a laminated piece of paper. Many schools attempting to reshape themselves have begun by articulating a written statement that articulates their vision. Unfortunately, many vision efforts have also ended with the written statement, which gets tucked away in wallets or posted on bulletin boards, soon to be papered over with routine announcements and fire-drill instructions.

Articulating a written statement can be an important part of formulating a vision, but the document should never be mistaken for the real thing. The real vision, says Robert Fritz, is apparent in the values and aspirations that employees display in their work:

> It also is seen by what disappoints these people and what they regret. We see it in their hope for the company, and their frustrations with it. We see it in their desire for the future, and their pride in their past accomplishments. We see it in the love they have for their organization.

What Vision Does

The right vision, says Nanus, has powerful and positive effects on the organization:

- It attracts commitment and energizes people.
- It creates meaning in workers' lives.
- It establishes a standard of excellence.
- It bridges the present and the future.

Warren Bennis and colleagues add that when organizations have a widely shared vision, employees better understand their own roles and "are transformed from robots blindly following instructions to human beings engaged in a creative and purposeful venture." Believing they can make a difference, workers are more likely to bring vigor and enthusiasm to their tasks, aligning human energies toward a common end.

A STIMULUS FOR CHANGE

The most important effect of vision may be as a stimulus for significant change. Fritz notes that in the absence of a strong shared sense of purpose, the different parts of an organization often work at cross-purposes. Progress in one direction stirs up forces that want to move in the opposite direction; the result is oscillation rather than advance. Only when everyone understands clearly which way the organization is moving can leaders establish priorities and coordinate efforts.

McDonald calls this "planning backwards." Temporarily setting aside concerns about state mandates, Carnegie units, and achievement tests, schools begin by visualizing, as concretely as possible, what they would like their graduates to be able to do. Then they ask, "How closely does today's reality match that ideal image?" An honest answer to that question will point out where changes need to be made.

The need for a unifying vision is especially strong in school settings, which have often been portrayed as "isolationist cultures." In her study of teaching, Susan Moore Johnson (1990b) concluded:

> Strong norms of autonomy and privacy prevail among teachers. Creeping fears of competition, exposure of shortcomings, and discomfiting criticism often discourage open exchange, cooperation, and growth. Until teachers overcome such fears and actively take charge of their own professional relations, teaching will likely remain isolating work.

But even when teachers collaborate, they do not always grapple with fundamental issues. Studies of shared decision-making have found that teacher-led change often focuses on peripheral—even trivial—issues. Gary Griffin, in a series of discussions with teachers in restructuring schools, found that while they freely cooperated on schoolwide issues, the collaboration had not led them to question their own or others' classroom practices, in part because the professional norm was "live and let live." He concluded that nothing less than a wholesale shift in school culture would deeply affect classroom practice.

A clear vision offers a core of meaning that unambiguously expresses what it means to work in that school, thus providing a shared standard by which teachers can gauge their own efforts. According to one teacher in a school that had recently developed a vision, "People are speaking the same language, they have the same kinds of informal expectations for one another, more common ground" (Conley and colleagues).

Is Vision Worth the Effort?

For administrators caught up in the daily whirl of meetings, phone calls, and minicrises, vision may appear to be something of a luxury—a stimulating exercise for people with time on their hands. They lodge a variety of objections.

Objection 1: *Vision is impractical.* This objection sees vision as a kind of armchair philosophy—mentally stimulating, but not anchored to the real world. The hard-edged reality of institutional life has little room for utopian musings.

Response: This complaint may result from an overemphasis on vision statements, which do sometimes indulge in rather grandiose language. But while the statement is an important step, it is far from the whole story. Ultimately, vision is as vision does—it lives or dies through thousands of small, daily actions of a kind that are highly practical. (Indeed, some schools have found they were practicing their vision long before they arrived at a formal statement.) Formulating a vision is a reminder of why the institution exists, and it leads people to seek out the actions that will bring the vision a little closer to reality.

Objection 2: *Vision is unnecessary.* Let's be candid: lack of vision is not the kind of hot-button issue that gets principals in trouble. A careless contract violation will bring a quick visit from the union rep; rowdiness on the playground will bring phone calls from the PTA; declining test scores will bring questions from the board. But lack of vision is seldom commented on and almost never acted on; when leaders are accused of lacking vision, it usually just means the critic wishes to dignify an existing grudge. Many principals seem to get along quite nicely without vision.

Response: This criticism overlooks the difference between short-term trouble and long-term trouble. Lack of a vision may not start any immediate fires, but it will provide a lot of kindling. Schools are always reflections of society, and today's society is in the midst of what consultant Peter Drucker (1994) calls the greatest transformation in history. Schools that fail to respond aggressively to these changes may look around in five or ten years and find that they have become unmanageable—or perhaps just irrelevant.

David Mathews argues that the public is on the verge of giving up on the school system. Unthinkable? Recall what happened to the Soviet Union: an intimidating "evil empire" in 1985, it was gone by 1990. We now know that it had passed the point of no return by 1985; only the force of social habit kept it going longer and kept observers from realizing it. Schools may not yet be in a similar position, but administrators who don't look beyond today's problems may find that tomorrow's problems have increased geometrically.

Objection 3: *Vision is dangerous.* Schools serve a diverse and contentious public that hangs together only by politely pretending that differences don't exist. Discussing vision brings those differences to the surface, reminding participants that their assumptions and values are not shared by everyone. The result may be an ideologically driven battle that openly divides the community. (This is one reason outcome-based education is so controversial; by making the school's intentions explicit, it stirs the passion of critics who object to publicly sanctioning goals they find offensive.)

Response: This objection has some validity. The divisions are real enough, and schools do have a tendency to seek out the lowest common denominator that will offend the fewest people. Developing a vision threatens to destroy this hard-won equilibrium.

But vision does not create divisions, it simply brings them to the surface. Left alone, these unstated disagreements act as a drag on the system, simmering for long periods and then erupting into sudden crisis. Parents may complain about a textbook not just because of any particular content but because of a more general fear that the school may undermine the values taught at home. Without any context for discussing the issues openly, anxiety becomes protest.

While vision does entail risks, it also offers a forum for dealing calmly with differences. Many schools have been able to work through the disagreements productively, never reaching unanimity, but achieving enough of a a consensus to move ahead.

Objection 4: *Vision requires visionaries.* School leaders commonly assume vision requires a visionary—someone who operates in an exalted state of hyperawareness. (Advocates of vision usually cite as their models people like Martin Luther King, Jr., Lee Iacocca, Bill

Gates, and Moses. Even on their best days, few school leaders would put themselves in that class.) Teachers and administrators live in a practical, down-to-earth world, and most don't have the training and inclination to be great visionaries.

Response: Ordinary schools have used vision effectively, depending on only their own resources and personnel. Fortunately, it turns out that leaders need not be capable of personally generating all kinds of futuristic ideas. There are plenty of good ideas floating around in the public domain, available to anyone willing to run with them.

What *is* required of leaders is nurturing vision wherever it can be found—in teachers, students, and parents—and persuading the school community to commit itself to big ideas. Roland Barth says vision already lives in the hearts of all educators. What it needs is a leader who will recognize it, empower it, and do the hard work of translating it into organizational reality.

THE LEADER'S ROLE

Recent scholars of leadership have been almost unanimous in declaring vision to be one of the essential attributes of the leader. Bennis and colleagues write:

> If there is a spark of genius in the extraordinary manager at all, it must lie in this transcending ability, a kind of magic, to assemble—out of all the variety of images, signals, forecasts and alternatives—a clearly articulated vision of the future that is at once simple, easily understood, clearly desirable, and energizing.

Howard Gardner describes this genius as the ability to relate a story that provides meaning to the lives of followers, a story in which the leader and followers are principal characters. "Together, they have embarked on a journey in pursuit of certain goals, and along the way and into the future, they can expect to encounter certain obstacles or resistances that can be overcome."

PREREQUISITES OF VISIONARY LEADERSHIP

Visionary leadership seems to entail some special challenges:

1. *The leader must "have" the vision.* That is, he or she must understand it well enough to tell if the school is moving in the right

direction. Richard Elmore and colleagues, after careful analysis of schools making serious reform efforts, found that claims of radical change were often premature: the "bold vision" turned out to be the old paradigm dressed up in new clothes. The researchers concluded that teaching habits were complex and deeply rooted, not likely to be changed merely by declaring a vision and fiddling with organizational structure. Leaders must be able to recognize the deep implications of the vision and resist the temptation to declare victory after the first few incremental changes.

2. *The leader must be deeply committed to the vision.* Researchers who have studied vision development in schools are virtually unanimous in stressing the difficulty and long-range nature of the process. Most assert that it takes a minimum of three to five years for the change to become established, and there are some suggestions that serious change may require a decade or more.

Clearly, vision is not for those with faint heart or short attention span. Career-minded leaders looking to score a quick success and then move on should seek other projects. Leaders who expect to leave should devote attention to building structures that will sustain the process after they are gone.

3. *The leader must be both directive and facilitative.* Getting a school to develop a new vision requires forceful action, energetic marketing, and occasional brow-beating; it simply doesn't happen by itself. In that sense the leader is the guardian of the vision. Yet the vision is never the leader's property. To be successful it must be owned by everyone in the organization, and the leader must be ready to step aside and let others take the central role, even if it means the original vision will be modified.

4. *The leader must be able to institutionalize the vision.* No matter how much excitement is created in the initial stages of vision development, the effort will eventually wither unless the full resources of the institution are put behind it. Leaders must be able to make the necessary changes in structure, reallocate resources, and devise ways to assess progress.

5. *The leader must live the vision in thought, word, and deed.* Visionaries do not just communicate their dreams in so many words, says Gardner; "they convey their stories by the kinds of lives they themselves lead." This is especially true for schools, where teachers are often highly sensitive to the social and emotional climate. If the

vision is inclusiveness and self-esteem, then the principal must embody those ideals when dealing with teachers. If the vision sees students as self-directed learners, principals must see faculty as self-directed learners. One teacher, interviewed by Lynn Liontos, made an explicit connection between the principal's behavior and classroom teaching:

> Students have to learn to use their own minds and be creative and do problem-solving on their own. So what teachers really need to be doing is to show kids how to become learners themselves, so that they can then chart their own paths. And I think essentially what Bob [the principal] is doing is modeling that approach to teachers, who may then pick up on it and use it with students.

In short, when teachers *experience* the vision they are better able to *apply* the vision.

WHO SHOULD TAKE THE LEAD?

School systems are multilevel organizations with multiple leaders, so it's reasonable to ask: Whose responsibility is the vision? Is it the job of the person at the top, something to be formulated by the superintendent and passed down to all schools? Or is it a local issue, something best left to building principals?

Judging from current practice, there seems to be little consensus. Sometimes the vision is formulated at the district level and all schools are expected to adhere to it. Sometimes the district vision sets out certain essentials but allows schools to develop their own visions within those limitations. Some districts use a laissez-faire approach, leaving vision up to each school.

District involvement is usually based on the belief that school boards, as the ultimate policy setters, should create or at least endorse the long-range direction for the district. Yet schools within the same district may have very different histories, constituencies, and cultures; a one-size-fits-all vision is unlikely to be effective. In addition, crafting and maintaining a vision requires extensive reflecting, experimenting, and negotiating, a process best done by small face-to-face groups.

A reasonable compromise is for district-level leadership to establish a framework and provide support for vision-building, but without trying to control the outcome. As John Dewey suggested long ago, the best use of large administrative units is to create environments in which smaller communities can flourish.

To guide and support vision-building by each school, school boards and superintendents may want to take three steps:

1. The district can develop a basic vision that sets out the core beliefs and aspirations of the district. At the very least, this broad vision provides a model for schools within the district; it also conveys a unifying message that reminds participants of what holds them together. District visions should be broadly stated, communicating core values but allowing plenty of room for variations. (Appendix A provides an example of what one district has done to establish a framework for vision.)

2. The district can require that each school has a vision, without dictating the details of that vision. At times it may be appropriate to require schools to address certain issues constituting a districtwide problem, but this should be done with restraint.

3. The district can provide guidance and resources to schools pursuing their visions. Too often, the central office is perceived as an obstacle to change instead of the superb resource for local schools that it could be. Conley notes that, in restructuring schools, central-office administrators are "boundary spanners," able to move freely among schools and in the community at large. They can bring together like-minded educators from different schools; build support for change in the larger community; and point school leaders to resources and strategic alliances.

Visionary leadership can arise anywhere, from superintendents, principals, teachers, and parents. However, this book is premised on the assumption that vision will succeed or fail at the school level, and that the person most responsible is the principal.

Wise leaders will look for a broad base of participation and will seek vision from all corners and put it to work for the school's benefit. But it remains the principal's responsibility.

TWO

DEVELOPING PERSONAL VISION

Where do visions come from? We have few detailed accounts of their creation, but all the available evidence suggests that they do not arrive full-grown, snatched out of the ether by some mystical process. There are no one-minute formulas for vision.

Research suggests that we begin the search by looking inward. While we often talk about "the school's vision," it is always *people* who have the vision; the school merely serves as a lens that focuses their beliefs, values, and insights. Before there is a vision, there must be people who *have* vision—people who can see the implications of their values and beliefs, not only today but projected into the future. This chapter examines the knowledge, skills, and attitudes that lead to vision.

The Foundations

Stephen Covey and colleagues associate vision with passion, a sustained energy that "taps into the deep core of who we are and what we are about." A compelling vision is not the result of a tidy intellectual exercise but is woven into the fabric of our lives. This section examines three basic elements of personal vision: values, thought processes, and the ability to link past, present, and future.

Values

Purpose is at the heart of every vision, and purpose is always a product of some belief system. According to Robert Starratt, this system contains bedrock assumptions about living, learning, and being human that "are to an organization what solar energy is to photosynthesis: they fuel the whole enterprise; they energize the other levels of the institution." Yet they may be so deeply rooted that they are taken for granted and not easily accessible. This is especially true of what Starratt calls myths—the fundamental meanings by which people make sense out of their lives, the daily assumptions that keep their world hanging together. (As Starratt uses the term, *myth* does not imply any skepticism about the truthfulness of a belief.)

Most people, for example, assume the world has a moral order, that some actions are proper and others are not. Most people likewise assume that they can influence the world around them. There are also myths about community, national identity, our relationship to the natural world, and the dignity of work.

And there are educational myths:

- The purpose of schooling is to prepare students for work.
- Teachers who have more knowledge of the subject will be more successful.
- The current generation knows what the next generation will need to be successful.
- Students learn more in school than they would without school.

Starratt suggests that a good deal of vision consists of bringing these deep beliefs to the surface, where they can be examined, critiqued, and enriched.

Linda Sheive and Marian Schoenheit found that the administrators they studied invariably linked their visions with their sense of values. At some point in their careers, those values collided with organizational realities, bringing the vision into sharp focus. One superintendent put it this way:

> It happens when you are deeply committed and it appears that outside forces constrict you. It is an irritant. Just like with an oyster, you create a pearl around the grain of irritation.

Many leaders shrug off that kind of conflict as just one of the annoyances inherent in organizational life. Leaders with vision, however, recognize the implications of the conflict, bring it to the surface, and use it as a stimulus to create something new.

Developing vision, then, is an act with fundamentally moral implications, especially for educational leaders. Schools constitute a "public trust," representing the hopes of an entire community for the next generation. Schooling is always an answer to the question, What kind of people should our children be?

Thus, leaders with vision must grapple with some imposing questions:

- How can we best serve our students?

- How can schools contribute to social justice?

- What kinds of human relationships should we be cultivating?

- What ethical principles should we be teaching?

These are not small issues, nor is it easy to articulate answers. But those with vision make an effort, however fumbling, to do so. Activities 1, 2, and 3 provide exercises to examine your basic values.

Activity 1

IDENTIFYING YOUR CORE VALUES

Long before you were a school leader, you were a human being with all the strengths, weaknesses, desires, and values of the average person. You still are. The beliefs you formed in childhood and the lessons you've learned from life are a part of what you try to do at school.

Completing these sentences may provide insights into the basic values that motivate you. The results of this activity, combined with Activity 2, will be a good predictor of your educational vision.

1. What our society needs most is....

2. What our society does best is...

3. The worst thing one person can do to another is...

4. A good citizen is someone who...

5. I will consider my life well-spent if...

6. What angers me more than anything is...

7. The most important lesson my parents ever taught me was...

8. A good human being is someone who...

9. The most important thing my teachers ever taught me was...

10. The greatest legacy I can leave my children is...

Activity 2

YOUR EDUCATIONAL PLATFORM

Numerous students of educational leadership have pointed to the principal's values as a key element in building visions (and, for that matter, in governing most of what the principal does). Collectively, these beliefs constitute an educational platform (Starratt). Starratt notes that the platforms of leaders tend to be visible more in their actions than in any formal statement, but suggests that brief written exercises can be helpful. This exercise elaborates on his suggestion.

Complete the following open-ended statements:

1. Students learn best when....

2. Classroom learning ought to emphasize...

3. The three most important qualities for teachers to have are....

4. Students are prepared for life when they...

5. The most valuable course in the curriculum is........because.........

6. The one compromise I would never make is......

7. The thing I most want students in my school to learn is.....

8. Teachers deserve to be fired when.....

9. I know we've failed when I see a student who....

10. When I leave this school, the one thing I want to be able to say about it is.....

Just completing the statements may be revealing, but they can also be further analyzed:

1. In the past few months, what actions have I taken to live up to these values?

2. Would a visitor to my school be able to guess how I completed these statements?

3. What steps could I take to bring these values closer to realization?

Activity 3

THE OYSTER EXERCISE

Abstract questions of philosophy can be intimidating, partly because they are so expansive, partly because they remind us these issues have been debated for 2000 years without a final resolution.

Thus it may be easier to start with small issues. This exercise is built around the insight of a superintendent whose vision originated as "grains of irritation" (Sheive and Schoenheit).

The goal is simply to identify sources of irritation and conflict that may indicate a clash between your implicit vision and the way the organization is actually run. Within the past month, what are the incidents or issues that have triggered feelings of annoyance, frustration, or even anger? Just list them before doing any analysis. (If you can't remember, it might be worthwhile to keep a daily log for a week or two, and then do the exercise.)

Then examine the ones that came to mind most quickly. First, try to determine exactly what it was that annoyed you. In some cases it may just have been a fleeting incident without long-range implications—the educational equivalent of a traffic jam. Other cases may be more significant (sometimes you can tell because the same type of incident keeps showing up). For example:

- A feeling of inadequacy after a teacher evaluation may mean that current practice is not living up to your beliefs.

- Annoyance at low parent turnout for conferences may reflect dismay because of your belief that parents should be involved with their children's education.

- Anger over a board member's criticism of your school's test scores may be triggered in part by the belief that standardized tests are a poor way of measuring student progress.

Then try to build around the irritation. If you could do things your way, how might those incidents be avoided? What would you want to show the board as evidence that students were learning? For that matter, how do you know? By going through this process a number of times, you may begin to build up a fairly concrete picture of your ideal school.   *(continued on next page)*

(continued from previous page)

One caution: the purpose of the exercise is not to solve particular problems. (Sometimes dwelling on the negative leads to a "fix-it" mentality in which the vision never gets a chance to breathe.) One way of avoiding this problem is to begin with the pearls. As you go through the day, keep track of the moments that really make you feel good about being associated with this school. Why are these moments so satisfying? What has led to them? How might they be spread? Each such pearl is a kind of minivision that connects with your deepest beliefs.

THOUGHT PROCESSES

Kenneth Leithwood and colleagues (1994) note that good leaders are good thinkers: they can interpret the situation, define problems, and figure out appropriate solutions. These skills are especially critical for "swampy problems," where the issues are not well defined and few precedents exist. In addition, expert principals know the values that motivate them, are less likely to consider obstacles as impassable, and are confident in their ability to make progress.

But this is a researcher's distillation of the process. Principals' thinking is always embedded in a dizzying flow of events, encounters, and decisions, and "is not something that they are consciously aware of; it is something habitually beneath the surface of their decisions and responses" (Starratt).

At times, however, this stream of thought needs to be brought to the surface. For example, when visionary leaders survey their school, they must be able to diagnose a problem thoughtfully rather than just using the most obvious or conventional explanation. Thus, poor attendance at parent conferences can easily be blamed on "parent apathy," while a closer look might show it to be the result of parents feeling uncomfortable in the school environment or being uncertain about the purpose of conferences. The implications for vision would be very different.

Similarly, good leaders are able to see their schools holistically. Citing the work of management expert Chris Argyris, Starratt says that some leaders routinely do single-loop learning; that is, problems are treated as separate, unrelated entities. Leaders merely assess the situation, pick a strategy, evaluate the results, and move on. By contrast, double-loop learning recognizes how the problem fits into the larger context of institutional dynamics. For example, when a teacher is performing poorly, the surface problem is finding a way to improve instruction, but any attempted solution will also have implications for student learning, the teacher's career, relations with the union, and the value system of the school. Double-loop learning leads to a better understanding of the institution as a whole.

Reflection

The kind of thoughtfulness described above results in part from the leader's expertise and familiarity with his or her school. However, there are many skillful leaders who don't get to this level because they don't cultivate the habit of reflection.

Reflection may seem a luxury for principals, who are always caught up in a whirlwind of activities and problems. Where will the time come from? If reflection is defined as serene monastic contemplation, the dilemma is probably unsolvable. However, Starratt argues that reflective practice can be built into the daily routine.

Principals, like teachers, rely less on theory than on intuition derived from experience. A problem arises; it seems to be the same kind of problem that occurred last month; and the tactic that worked then is used again (Arthur Blumberg). Effective principals tend to monitor their strategies, consciously asking how well they are working. Visionary principals dig even deeper. "Why am I doing this? Does this activity or approach help accomplish the things that are most worth doing?" Such questions bridge the gap between "doing things right" and "doing the right things."

This kind of questioning can be done on the fly, and while it does not usually yield immediate answers, it tends to take root, surfacing spontaneously in otherwise idle moments, such as the daily commute. (Studies of problem-solving have found that the combination of conscious thought with a subconscious "incubation period" is often highly effective.)

Moreover, reflection feeds on itself. When principals begin asking reflective questions aloud (for example, at faculty meetings), they often get reflective questions back, which in turn forces them to do still more thinking.

Creative Thinking

Beyond reflective analysis, visionary thinking also has an element of imagination that isn't captured by straightforward logic. Visions, after all, deal with things that don't yet exist. Margaret Wheatley cites Albert Einstein's belief that "no problem can be solved from the same consciousness that created it. We must learn to see the world anew." Economist Hazel Henderson exemplifies this kind of zestful embrace of life, which she compares to a five-year-old's wide-eyed question about the meaning of life:

> I've had that question in me all my life. And I love it! It makes every day fresh. If you can keep that question fresh and remember what that was like when you were a child and you looked around and you looked at, say, trees and you forgot that you knew the word tree—you've never seen anything like that before. And you haven't named anything. And you haven't routinized your perceptions at all. And then every morning you wake up and it's like the dawn of creation. (Quoted in Mihaly Csikszentmihalyi)

Csikszentmihalyi, who has studied creativity for most of his career, recognizes several different types, including the kind of everyday playfulness and freshness of perception that make some people such enjoyable companions. However, most of his work has concentrated on creative effort that leads to new ideas being accepted by the culture (which is exactly the challenge facing the visionary principal).

He has found many contradictions. Creative people are at times passive, at other times assertive; in some ways very smart, in other ways naive; in some ways playful, in other ways highly disciplined. They show great virtuosity in being able to switch back and forth as the situation demands.

More significantly, he concludes (as have others) that creativity is built on expertise: "a genuinely creative accomplishment is almost never the result of a sudden insight, a lightbulb flashing in the dark, but comes after years of hard work." At the same time, creative people are able to step beck from their expertise and see a subject with fresh eyes.

Csikszentmihalyi's advice for developing creativity includes:

- Be open to new experiences—try to be surprised by something every day.

- Start doing more of what you love and less of what you hate.
- Look at problems from as many perspectives as possible.
- Keep challenging yourself with increasingly complex issues.

Warren Bennis and colleagues urge leaders to cultivate intuitive thinking that breaks conventional mindsets. They suggest that such thinking is best done in relaxed, receptive states of mind, and that it relies more on visual images than abstract language. For example, principals could take a mental walk through their ideal school. Strolling through the corridors, what will they see? What are students working on? How are they working? What's on the walls?

Vision *sees*, and in the seeing it becomes real. Reflective thinking may lead us to what we think works best; intuitive thinking leads us to what we most desire. Together, they form a powerful visionary tool.

The Entrepreneurial Mindset

Ideas alone don't change organizations—actions do. The great innovators—the people who really change the world—are those who take a creative idea and put it to work. For example, friendly computers (with easy-to-understand graphical commands and mouse control) were invented at a Xerox laboratory, but it was Apple Computer that took the idea and revolutionized the way people used computers. The most ingenious idea in the world will do no good unless a leader is enterprising enough to act on it.

Entrepreneurship does not come easily to public institutions. Peter Drucker (1985) says, "The forces that impede entrepreneurship and innovation in a public-service institution are inherent in it, integral to it, inseparable from it." One reason is that public agencies have moral rather than economic goals, so their purposes tend to be both ambitious and ambiguous. (For example, many schools define their mission as "meeting the needs of all students.") The lack of a simple yardstick (such as profit) makes it easy to lavish attention on inputs rather than measure results; the nobility of the goal makes one feel virtuous for even trying.

According to Drucker, entrepreneurs have a number of qualities. They are constantly monitoring performance, looking for discrepancies between what is and what ought to be. They are opportunistic:

an unexpected event is seen not as a problem or barrier but as an opportunity to learn. And, above all, they are ready to move quickly—today's opportunities are likely to be fleeting because of rapidly changing conditions.

Visionary school leaders also have this entrepreneurial quality. They operate less from a detailed blueprint and more from a built-in compass that allows them to sense and seize opportunities. While business entrepreneurs look for market niches, principal-entrepreneurs look for creative niches, situations in which an adventurous teacher can be connected with the resources and encouragement needed to launch an experiment. In this way, the vision is advanced a little at a time.

TIME-BINDING

A number of thinkers have characterized human beings as "time-binders." That is, in a single action they can combine an appreciation of the past, an understanding of the present, and a concern for the future. (Thus a motorist refills the gas tank because he sees the gas gauge at a certain level, recalls what happened the last time it reached this point, and wants to avoid getting stranded on the highway again.) This same capacity—developed to a high degree—seems to be a characteristic of visionary leaders.

Past

For most school leaders, time is compressed into the here-and-now, as constant demands for attention keep their eyes firmly on the daily to-do list. Sometimes an approaching deadline forces a brief look ahead, but contemplation of the past seems a luxury.

Yet visionary leaders have an acute sense of history. Martin Luther King, Jr. is best remembered for the forward-looking "I have a dream," but what gave his speech emotional weight were the centuries of history invoked by the climactic, "Free at last! Free at last! Thank God Almighty, free at last!" King's vision was driven by history, and it showed up in his allusions, his metaphors, and even the rhythmic cadence of his language.

It seems paradoxical, but visions that move people forward almost always connect them with some part of their past. The reason is simple: without continuity, life would be a jumble of unrelated events rather than a coherent journey. This is why so many people explain themselves with a story that tells how they have come to be where they are, and where they go from here. (A person with no past—an amnesiac—is a person with no future: no plans, no dreams, no phone calls to make.)

In some cases, visions will reaffirm the existing path, holding out hope of doing better what we've been doing all along. The capsulized story is, "I have continually sought new ways of meeting student needs and have continually improved, and will continue to improve." Another common story is, "I came into teaching with all kinds of idealism but learned the system doesn't appreciate creativity." Here the vision is likely to be regarded as a type of liberation. Another common story is the Legend of the Golden Age: "In a far-off enchanted time, education worked: students came to school motivated, parents were supportive, and people appreciated teachers." Here the vision is likely to point "back to the future."

No matter how radical the vision, it never completely escapes history; the future always incorporates the past. At one level, all individuals have a personal history, a unique set of experiences that has shaped who they are and what they believe. In particular, they have an educational history: the sum total of their experiences with learning (in and outside of school). Much of what people believe about education is rooted in their own learning experiences. (Activity 4 will help you to reflect on the lessons of your own experience.)

Second, every community (nation, city, or school) has a shared history, a common set of experiences that become part of the psychological makeup of those who work or live there.

Part of the leader's job, then, is to understand how stakeholders see the school's history, and to find ways to build on the positive elements in that history. Visions work best when they offer a bridge from the past to the future.

Present

While visionaries obviously have a strong orientation to the future, they are also firmly planted in the present, with a strong sense of reality. They continually scan the environment for signs that the school is achieving its mission.

Visionary leaders see things on both a large scale and a small scale. On the one hand, leaders must know their organizations,

Activity 4

PERSONAL EDUCATIONAL HISTORY

Many educators can testify how their own experiences as learners shaped their beliefs about teaching:

- A class with an inspiring teacher created a mental model of good teaching that lasts a lifetime.

- A traumatic experience led to the vow, "When I'm a teacher, I'll never..."

- Making the rank of Eagle Scout revealed capacities never before suspected and showed the payoff for unremitting hard work.

These experiences often lie close to our personal education vision. Becoming fully aware of them can help bring that vision to the surface.

The activity involves writing a narrative of your own educational experiences. "Educational" should be interpreted broadly—it includes learning in and out of school. The simplest approach is starting at birth and working forward chronologically, but the format is open-ended, so whatever seems most natural is best.

In the process, you might want to consider the following questions:

1. What learning experiences have had the biggest impact on you? What experiences have been most useful in the long run?

2. Under what conditions have you learned most effectively?

3. When you think of "good teaching," which of your teachers come to mind? Why?

4. What was your worst moment in school? Your best moment?

5. What's the most important lesson you learned outside of school? Could this lesson have been learned in school?

6. What do you wish your schools and teachers had done differently?

inside and out, keeping a finger on the pulse of the hundreds of daily transactions that make up institutional life. On the other hand, they also must see the big picture, recognizing social and cultural trends that affect the institution's work.

Principals keep track in a number of ways. The simplest way is engagement—what some have called "management by walking around." Cruising the hallways and poking one's nose in classrooms will yield a wealth of detailed information about the school.

There are also formal indicators: achievement test scores, SAT results, state tests, disciplinary referrals, at-risk data, faculty surveys, attendance reports, and PTA minutes. This information flows across the principal's desk in a fairly steady stream, but is often underused. (Activity 5 provides a brief checklist. A more comprehensive survey can be found in Kenneth Leithwood and Robert Aitken.)

Schools are also part of a larger social "ecosystem" of institutions and individuals interacting in ways that are sometimes helpful, sometimes antagonistic. The public school ecosystem includes state agencies, parent and community sentiments, textbook publishers, colleges and universities, teacher-education programs, and job-market requirements. In addition, schools feel the effects of changes in family structures and social mores.

This ecosystem was remarkably stable for much of the twentieth century. Stakeholders understood their roles and carried out their business in a predictable way. Today, however, this system is under severe stress:

- The public has lost faith that schools are doing the job.

- An aging population is increasingly reluctant to fund education at the traditional levels.

- Political pressure is pushing schools toward a free-market model.

- Knowledge is becoming a commodity, with schools no longer the sole vendors.

- Schools cannot assume that families will fulfill their traditional roles in providing physical protection and emotional security.

- Education is spilling over the old boundaries, becoming a lifelong process that can take place anywhere, any time.

School leaders who track these developments are better prepared to move the school forward proactively. For example, some schools, seeing the increased psychosocial needs of children, have redesigned

Activity 5

VITAL INDICATORS

Staying in touch with what's going on requires systematic monitoring of the school and its environment, using whatever information is available. The list of questions below is designed to provide a quick snapshot of the school's "vital indicators." (Those interested in doing more systematic monitoring should check Leithwood and Aitken's *Making Schools Smarter: A System for Monitoring School and District Progress*.)

Most of these questions generate information that is fairly objective (though not always at hand). The last few questions are more subjective, but worth pondering.

1. Overall, standardized test scores are approximately at the _____ percentile.
2. Performance on other tests (SATs, mandated state exams, local competency tests) is good/poor/so-so.
3. In recent years, test scores have been rising/dropping/staying about the same.
4. The absenteeism rate is running about _____ percent. In recent years, this rate has been rising/dropping/staying about the same.
5. In a typical freshman class, about ___ percent drop out before graduation.
6. The percentage of graduating students who go on to college is around _____.
7. The number of serious disciplinary actions (suspension/ expulsion) is around ____ a month.
8. In general, disciplinary referrals of all types have been rising/ dropping/staying about the same in recent years.
9. The number of teachers on staff who are currently teaching out of their major area is _____.
10. The overall student GPA in this school is around _____. In recent years, this has been rising/dropping/staying about the same.
11. The percentage of students eligible for free hot lunches is around_____. In recent years, this number has been rising/dropping/staying about the same.
12. The percentage of students who are considered "at risk" is about ____. In recent years, this number has been rising/ dropping/staying about the same.

13. The job outlook for students in this district is good/poor/so-so.

14. The percentage of parents who show up for conferences is about _____. In recent years, this number has been rising/dropping/staying about the same.

15. The percentage of parents who volunteer in the classroom (or other activities) is around_____. In recent years, this number has been rising/dropping/staying about the same.

16. Financial support for schools in this district is good/poor/so-so. In recent years it has been rising/dropping/staying about the same.

17. The percentage of school-age children in this community who attend public schools is around_____. In recent years, that number has been rising/dropping/staying about the same.

18. Real estate agents in this neighborhood love it/hate it/don't care when prospective buyers ask about the quality of schools.

19. The number one concern of parents in this school seems to be _____.

20. The number one concern of teachers in this school seems to be_____.

21. The number one concern of students in this school seems to be____.

22. The greatest external danger to this school comes from_____.

23. The greatest internal danger to this school comes from_____.

24. The greatest strength of this school is_____.

25. The one thing that would improve this school the most is_____.

26. The thing that makes me proudest of this school is_____.

Reflections: Perhaps the most important questions that can be asked about this information are: In what direction is this school headed? Is it a healthy one? Does it match my sense of where the school ought to be going?

themselves as "full-service" institutions, cooperating with social-service agencies to provide comprehensive services under one roof.

What gives all this information visionary potential is the attitude of the leader, who does not just file it and forget it, but instead keeps up a steady interrogation of the school's performance. What do these data say about our current performance? Are we moving in the direction we want? Does the information show that our mission is being fulfilled?

An Eye to the Future

One obstacle to vision is the natural tendency to assume that the near future (five to ten years) will be much like the present. But the environment is always changing, and a vision that fails to anticipate change is a vision that won't have much impact. (If a buggy-whip company in 1905 set a ten-year vision of making the world's best buggy-whip, fulfilling the goal would be pretty much irrelevant.)

John Hoyle points out that the future is not something that simply shows up unannounced a few years down the road; instead, it is something that is created by the actions we take today:

> We must assume that we can change our course as a captain would steer a boat to the harbor or down a rapidly moving river. Change must occur early if the boat is to arrive safely at the mouth of the river. We are often tied to a successful past, and when trouble strikes, we are unprepared to make changes in time to avoid running aground.

"Future sight" seems especially important now, at a time of unprecedented social change. Drucker (1994) puts it bluntly, saying that work, society, and government in developed economies are "qualitatively and quantitatively different not only from what they were in the first years of this century but also from what has existed at any other time in history: in their configurations, in their processes, in their problems, in their structures." He believes the changes will not peak by the year 2000.

So a reasonable person could anticipate that schools in ten years will find themselves in an environment that differs noticeably from today's world. But what will the changes be? Does vision require predicting the future?

Peter Schwartz, an expert in long-range planning, says prediction is not the point. No one can know the future with certainty; instead, the goal is to increase awareness of possibilities. Having considered what *might* happen, a leader is better prepared for what *does* happen.

Imagine, for a moment, the following scenarios:

- High-quality self-contained educational programs become available on the Internet, easily downloaded for a small fee.

- The emergence of voucher systems places schools in a highly competitive market.

- The number of high-risk students grows dramatically.

- New technology permits students to participate in "virtual classes" anywhere in the world while sitting at home.

- Parents become insistent on using a back-to-the-basics approach, with a heavy emphasis on test scores.

- The town's major employer closes down.

- A major high-tech company establishes an office that will attract thousands of well-educated workers to the community.

- Increased demand for adult education leads to schools being open fifteen hours a day for all kinds of courses.

Obviously, no one knows which (if any) of these scenarios will actually unfold, yet any of them could. Exploring the possibilities serves several purposes. First, some important trends may become obvious once we take the trouble to look for them. The enrollment decline of the 1970s and 1980s was perfectly predictable, yet many schools were caught unaware, forcing them to lay off teachers and close schools in a crisis atmosphere. In the 1990s, demographic projections show a continuing increase in student diversity, especially in populations that schools have been least successful with. The impact may not affect all schools equally, but educators ignore the trend at their own risk.

Second, even those possibilities that never come to pass may stimulate useful thinking. For example, the prospect of a high-tech boom is wishful thinking for most communities, but simply asking the question generates some interesting thoughts. Aside from the obvious issue of facilities, the influx of well-educated workers into the community might raise some curricular questions. Would the newcomers demand more academically challenging classes and a stronger college-prep program? Where *is* our curriculum? Whose needs are we meeting? Even if the high-tech company never comes here, our children will be growing up in a high-tech world—will they be ready for it?

Looking to the future takes us out of the here-and-now, reminding us that our best efforts today may fall far short tomorrow. (Activities 6 and 7 offer two ways of looking at the future.)

Activity 6

WHAT IF....?

Stan Davis and Jim Botkin point out that knowledge is quickly becoming a commodity, a consumer item available at relatively low cost from many vendors. Whereas knowledge once was primarily dispensed through books in special locations (schools and libraries), today learning can be done almost anywhere at any time using a variety of media: books, sound tapes, video tapes, television, CDs, electronic conferencing, and computers. Today "the education business" includes YMCAs, scout groups, business corporations, the military, private daycare centers, and a growing number of small entrepreneurs. Davis and Botkin argue that this poses a serious challenge to schools, which have never been in the business of creating knowledge, just delivering it.

SCENARIO: It is 2010, and the state has passed a "learning voucher" law that provides parents with vouchers that can be redeemed not just through schools but through any vendor providing appropriate educational experiences. Parents can choose to spend their money in a variety of places: a health class from the local "Y"; interactive online physics lessons produced by a world-class group of science teachers; and a "virtual-reality" social-studies seminar that brings together students from around the country.

Questions for reflection: In this scenario, what is the role of your school? What unique value-added contribution can it make to a child's education? What can it offer that parents would be willing to buy? What would you have to do now to start getting the school ready for the new situation?

Activity 7

DELPHI FORECASTING

The Delphi technique is a venerable forecasting method named after the oracle at Delphi, where the ancient Greeks would seek answers about their future. Of course, the exercise does not assume that anybody has such mystical powers, but it does assume that a representative, informed group of people can collectively provide insights into social and cultural trends.

The exercise asks you to invite a small group (6-8 participants) from outside the school (political leaders, parents, business people) and host a discussion of current trends in their domain. You should allow 1-2 hours, ideally in a congenial environment such as over lunch. Ask them to come having thought about these questions:

1. What current trends do you see that are changing the way you do business or carry out your responsibilities? (over the next decade)

2. How do those trends affect what you expect of schools?

The format is simple. Each person should be given a chance to talk about the questions, but beyond that it can be fairly unstructured. In most cases, a lot of exchange and cross-fertilization will be going on.

FINDING YOUR VISION

For beleaguered principals, sitting in the shadow of inbaskets stacked with concrete and mundane tasks, vision can seem abstract and nebulous. Administrators tend to see themselves as doers, not dreamers, taking pride in managing real-world complexities rather than speculating about hypothetical possibilities. Is it realistic to expect them to engage in what seems to be a very creative process? The answer is clearly "yes."

We can take a cue from fiction writers, who are often exasperated by fans who ask, "Where do you get your ideas?" Writers find the question difficult to answer. On the one hand, they certainly don't pull down an Idea Encyclopedia and pick a plot; on the other hand, they don't sit around in a trance-like state waiting for inspiration to strike. Rather, the best writers are engaged with life, keeping their eyes open for the dramas, characters, and oddities that make up human existence. At some point inspiration does bubble to the surface, but it would be wrong to say it comes out of nowhere.

Kouzes and Posner, arguing that intuition is "the wellspring of vision," claim there is nothing mystical about it. It is simply an accelerated mental process that reflects long experience and great expertise in a domain. An idea may seem to come out of nowhere, they say, but "it's the years of direct contact with a variety of problems and situations that equip the leader with unique insight. Listening, reading, smelling, feeling, and tasting the business—these tasks improve our vision." Thus the foundations of vision lie in everyday experience.

SMALL BEGINNINGS

In the beginning, say Kouzes and Posner, the grandest vision is only a glimmer of an idea, "a vague desire to do something that would challenge yourself and others." At this stage, the operative word is "possibility," not "probability." What counts is that it could happen, not that it is probable.

They cite the example of teacher Nolan Dishongh, who begins each year believing that each of his at-risk students wants to be a responsible, informed human being. At the beginning of the year, an objective observer might not see this as a likely outcome, but the fact that Dishongh sees the possibility increases the probability.

Roland Barth concedes that practitioners' visions are usually "deeply submerged, sometimes fragmentary, and seldom articulated.... But I am convinced the vision is there." Too often, he suggests, people begin their educational careers with a strong sense of idealism and "a 20/20 personal vision," only to have it collide with bureaucratic procedures and mandates. Most people learn to keep their visions in the closet in order to keep the discrepancy between real and ideal from being too painful.

So the first step is to get the vision out into the light where it can can be seen and become tangible. While the activities earlier in the chapter may have provided clues to your vision, it is important at this point to state the vision as clearly and concretely as possible.

One way is to write a short paragraph that begins, "I see students who...." When you visualize your future graduates, what knowledge, skills, and values do they have? What sort of relationships do they have with each other and the adults in their lives? Where are they headed? (When you're finished, you may want to write a corollary paragraph that begins, "I see teachers who...")

How do you know when you have it? First, it will feel "right." You can imagine your pride and satisfaction in turning out students like this, and you can recognize this vision in some of the actions you have already taken in your school.

Second, it will seem realistic. This is a tricky requirement, because it is all too easy to look at a dream and say, "Nah—not in this school." There are always dozens of obstacles that stand in the way. Those barriers become important later in the process, but at this point the goal is psychological realism. That is, your picture of future graduates should be true to your sense of their human potential. (Careful observers will see hints of that potential every day in students' thoughts, words, and deeds.)

Third, it will be succinct. John Kotter says, "If you cannot describe your vision to someone in five minutes and get their interest, you have more work to do in this phase of a transformation process."

Finally, even if it meets all these criteria, the vision is far from fully formed—and may never be complete. Karen Seashore Louis and Matthew Miles, after analyzing the experience of restructuring urban schools, concluded that visions ultimately become meaningful only when they are applied in real-world settings:

> "Visioning" is a dynamic process, no more a one-time event that has a beginning and an end than is planning. Visions are developed and reinforced from action, although they may have a seed that is based simply on hope.

GROWING THE VISION

The brief vision statement marks just the beginning of a long process. For the vision to become a robust presence in your life and the life of your school, it requires careful nurturing.

1. *Make it real by incorporating it into your everyday vocabulary and conversations.* Secret visions tend to have an air of unreality; they come alive only when shared with others. Going public feels risky:

Will others accept your vision? Will they roll their eyes and give each other funny looks? But taking the risk affirms your commitment to the vision, and, as others sense you're serious, their reactions will provide valuable feedback and will further challenge your own thinking.

2. *Determine the implications.* What would have to change for your vision to come true? New board policies? A different governance structure? Better teacher training? Improved home-school relationships? What kinds of structures and innovations would support the vision?

Fortunately, this process does not require reinvention of the wheel. Most visions do not depend on futuristic technology or new ideas, just a creative adaptation of well-known principles. Somewhere around the country are principals and teachers with a similar vision who have found a way of doing something about it. All that's needed is a good antenna:

- Journals like *Educational Leadership*, *NASSP Bulletin*, and *Principal* are filled with short, readable accounts of what schools are doing to improve their programs.

- Browsing the AskERIC database (http://ericir.syr.edu) will turn up a wealth of material.

- Participating in an online LISTSERV (such as ERIC's K12ADMIN list) will provide access to school leaders around the country.

- Your own faculty probably have all kinds of ideas that they haven't bothered mentioning because nobody asked.

3. *Begin acting on the vision.* As a school leader, you may want to build a shared vision (see chapter 4), but modelling your personal vision need not wait. Even small changes in policy and practice will affirm the vision and provide valuable feedback about implementation.

BLOCKS TO VISION

Sometimes, of course, the ideas don't come. In part this happens because the conservative, security-oriented side of human thinking dominates the expansive, novelty-seeking side (Csikszentmihalyi).

In part it happens because humans are such skillful learners. Without much conscious effort, they can take almost any kind of experience and transform it into a "lesson" that guides future behavior. Childhood is full of such lessons:

- When you hit people, they tend to hit back.

- Never hold a bee in your closed fist.

- If you can get Mom to say "Maybe," Dad will say "Yes."

- Being number one is the most important thing in the world.

On the whole, this is a useful ability that serves people well; it's hard to imagine getting through a day, much less life, without applying the lessons of experience. But once learned, a lesson is hard to unlearn, even when it is no longer relevant to a changing world. (Unfortunately, the lessons that have worked best in the past are the ones that are most likely to get us into trouble.)

Peter Senge refers to these lessons as "mental models." Everyone carries around pictures of how the world works, and normally we expect the world to continue working that way. Mental models often operate on a deep level; in fact, the stronger they are, the less likely they are to be conscious. In times of stability, they are highly productive tools; in times of upheaval, they can be major roadblocks to progress.

Some mental models pertain to organizational life:

- The master contract makes significant change almost impossible.

- We're stuck with the current grading system because parents want it.

- Leaders must be clear, consistent, and assertive about their expectations.

Some models deal with professional beliefs:

- Learning is best measured by the amount of content students know.

- Schools cannot be successful unless students feel good about themselves.

- Students cannot be motivated without grades.

And some models express deep attitudes about life and human nature:

- People respond well to trust.

- You can't predict the future.

- The more things change, the more they stay the same.

Models such as these usually have at least an element of truth (they are models because at some point in the past they worked). However, they don't apply at all times in all places, and because they are usually beneath the surface, they can prevent us from seeing the possibilities that exist.

How to escape the grip of these powerful preconceptions? Experts recommend a variety of approaches.

1. *Do something different.* When we spend each day in the same environment, preconceptions are easily reinforced or kept beneath the surface. This is especially true in schools, which have a well-established, comfortable rhythm. Taking a day to visit another school can challenge some of those preconceptions; observing as an outsider allows you to see with fresh eyes—and may lead to some rethinking about what happens at your school. Similarly, you could pick up a magazine you normally don't read or have lunch with students or spend a day shadowing a college admissions counselor.

2. *Talk to people "on the edge."* Wayne Burkan notes that most businesses prefer to talk with satisfied customers. But because they're satisfied, these people are unlikely to offer insights into the way the world is changing. Burkan says disgruntled customers (or maverick employees) are the ones business should be talking to, because their dissatisfaction is often the leading edge of important economic, social, and cultural trends.

Malcontents are never pleasant to talk to, but Burkan recommends seeking them out. In schools, candidates include parents who have withdrawn their children, teachers who are continually doing battle with the established curriculum, and that scruffy-looking group of smokers standing across the street from the school. Admittedly, some of these people will be operating from their own mistaken mental models, but they will provide a stiff challenge to our normal way of looking at things.

3. *Interrogate your assumptions.* Mental models are most dangerous when they deflect us from necessary change. At the very least, they should be brought out into the open. Try this exercise. Imagine a change you'd like to see but that you think is out of reach. Identify the reason it isn't likely to happen. Why do you say that? What is that position based on? Can you imagine circumstances under which it would not be true? (For example, if the goal is to transform the grading system, the obstacle may be "Parents won't accept it."

Probably this is based on previous attempts that failed because of parental resistance. But why did they resist? Do you actually know what they want in a grading system? Have they been asked? Those questions may open up new possibilities.)

Mental models are not the only blocks to vision. Bennis and colleagues suggest a number of others:

- Being too focused on daily routines. (The concreteness of the daily routine tempts one away from the more ambiguous challenge of developing a vision.)

- Wanting to be just one of the crowd. (A bold vision is risky; it calls attention to oneself and creates new expectations.)

- Flitting from one thing to the other. (Some people are overwhelmed by possibilities; in trying to cover everything, they end up without a clear focus on anything.)

- Reckless risk-taking. (Some leaders enjoy a high-wire act in which they are the stars.)

- Clinging to established principles to avoid ambiguity. (Creating a new future is filled with uncertainty; some leaders just tinker around the margins.)

- Being too open-minded. (Some leaders find it difficult to choose.)

- Believing you have all the answers. (In their hearts, some leaders simply don't believe that major change is needed.)

FINAL THOUGHTS

Despite the high-powered rhetoric that some people apply to vision, it is not the sole possession of brilliant, charismatic leaders. Some visions may be less eloquently stated than others; some may not range through time and space to capture the spirit of the age; some may not have the power to move a nation.

But it's enough if a vision expresses the needs and hopes of one school in one community—a goal that lies within the reach of school leaders. The next two chapters explain how the leader can move from personal vision to vision shared by the whole school.

THREE

PAVING THE WAY

Developing a vision for a school is not something to be done lightly; barging ahead recklessly is likely to result in failure (thereby increasing cynicism and diminishing confidence among teachers) or, at best, a "paper success" (with the vision statement plastered on every piece of paper in sight but otherwise cheerfully ignored). Kindling a vision can unleash powerful forces, threatening the existing order and making people aware of uncomfortable facts or philosophical disagreements. Unwary leaders may find themselves with a boiling pot and no way to turn down the heat.

While vision development is not always a systematic march toward the future (see chapter 4), it does require careful deliberation at each step. The first section of this chapter describes a preliminary readiness check for leaders who wish to develop or renew their school's vision. The second section discusses two strategic decisions that will shape the direction of the vision process: Who will lead? and Who will participate?

PRELIMINARY STEPS

Armchair visions—abstract musings about personal ideals—will always have a kind of detached quality until they are applied to actual school settings. Making that connection depends on a realistic perception of the school: its culture, its resources, and its community context. Visionary leaders know their institutions, and they tailor their actions accordingly.

KNOWING THE LIMITS

The first issue is the question of limits. Every school is a part of a larger system, subject to rules and regulations that may limit its freedom to innovate. The leader must thus determine: How free are we to reinvent ourselves? Are certain changes off limits? (Could we, for example, decide to operate our school from 10 a.m. until 5 p.m. or is the district's bus schedule sacred?) Will resources be available to put our ideas into effect? Is the union receptive to changes in teachers' work roles? Leaders who can't answer these questions would be well advised to move cautiously.

W. Patrick Dolan argues that major transformations are unlikely without "deep buy-in" from the board, superintendent, union, or anyone with effective veto power over the school's vision. Getting public, formal approval from these groups diminishes skepticism that "the system" won't permit real change.

Such explicit approval is not always available, of course. District officials are not always eager to encourage mavericks who may disrupt the bureaucratic machinery or upset a delicate political equilibrium. When the support is not forthcoming—or the principal is convinced it will not be given—there are still several alternatives. Sometimes central administrators are not willing to take the risk of publicly approving a proposal that sails off in uncharted directions, but will not object if the school quietly moves ahead. A participant in one elementary school's vision process said:

> Yes, the Associate Superintendent knew what we were doing and he relayed it to the Superintendent. And you know it wasn't publicized good or bad. They just allowed it... They let us go out on a limb. I wouldn't say that they fully supported us that first year, but they didn't tell us not to. (Marlene Johnson)

Some schools—especially those in large bureaucratic systems—have found merit in the adage, "It's easier to get forgiveness than permission." A school that makes changes quietly may find that no one notices. By the time the program gets big enough to attract attention, it may also be successful enough to withstand attack.

If nothing else, the principal must be ready to communicate the limits to faculty. Most teachers are pragmatists about the whims of higher authority and can adapt to these realities without disenchantment, as long as they haven't invested major energy in false assumptions.

In all cases, visionary principals must think politically, finding ways to finesse state laws, squeeze out resources, find allies, and negotiate informal understandings with the powers that be.

TAKING STOCK

One of the first lessons learned by every teacher is that no two classes are exactly alike; the lesson that worked beautifully in first hour may fall flat during second hour. The same is true of schools. Each has its own history, its own culture, its own personality. To launch a vision without knowing the school is a high-risk strategy.

Knowing the school requires asking the right questions. The principal can often answer these questions based on his or her knowledge of the school, but more objective data—such as survey results—may also help. (Several informal surveys appear in this chapter. However, as with all surveys of this type, caution should be used in interpreting the results. Surveys measure *perceptions*, not actual behaviors.)

1. *What values and beliefs guide decision-making in this organization?* Prevailing norms often determine attitudes toward the vision. For example, a faculty might be guided by these values (which are often unstated):

- Academic proficiency is the highest goal.
- Teachers never criticize other teachers' methods.
- Go along to get along.
- Above all, students should learn to believe in themselves.
- Parents should be an integral part of the school.
- Some students just can't learn.

These beliefs offer two kinds of clues to leaders. First, areas of strong consensus are often visions waiting to be articulated. At the very least, they provide a strong foundation that leaders can use in building commitment to a shared agenda. Thomas Chenoweth and James Kushman studied three principals who attempted to develop a vision initiated by the central office; all had some success, but the most effective principal made a point of showing teachers how the new vision was only an extension and elaboration of beliefs they already valued.

Second, the beliefs may point out areas of tension within an emerging vision. For example, teachers may embrace the value of home-school cooperation, yet express ambivalence about parental involvement on site councils. Awareness of these tensions allows leaders to anticipate potential difficulties as the vision develops. (See Survey 1: Assessing Teacher Beliefs. In addition, Activity 2 from chapter 2 can be adapted to provide insights about faculty beliefs.)

Survey 1

ASSESSING TEACHER BELIEFS

Respond to each statement on a scale from 1 (= "strongly disagree") to 5 (="strongly agree").

1. Schools require too much meaningless memorization.

    1————————2————————3————————4————————5

2. Systematic direct instruction should be at the heart of the educational process.

    1————————2————————3————————4————————5

3. Children would be better off if they could study the things *they* were interested in.

    1————————2————————3————————4————————5

4. Education should transmit the best of the human heritage—the time-tested knowledge, skills, and beliefs that are at the heart of human civilization.

    1————————2————————3————————4————————5

5. Learning is more meaningful if students can immediately use it to solve real-life problems.

    1————————2————————3————————4————————5

6. Academic learning—not personal and social development—should be the main goal of the school system.

    1————————2————————3————————4————————5

7. Students will do better if they are taught to rely on their own critical thinking rather than on the authority of others.

1————————2————————3————————4————————5

8. Students need an extensive stock of factual information before they can be creative thinkers.

1————————2————————3————————4————————5

9. Learning through active hands-on experience is more meaningful than learning through a textbook.

1————————2————————3————————4————————5

10. Although it's important to be open to diverse views, there *are* essential truths that ought to be taught to children.

1————————2————————3————————4————————5

11. Children have an instinctive understanding of their own needs, and in the long run they can be trusted to make wise choices about their own learning.

1————————2————————3————————4————————5

12. Civilization depends on literacy; reading and writing should be the main focus of the school curriculum.

1————————2————————3————————4————————5

13. Schools should emphasize cooperation rather than competition.

1————————2————————3————————4————————5

14. We should be pushing students harder to achieve more.

1————————2————————3————————4————————5

15. Students would be better off if we didn't give grades.

1————————2————————3————————4————————5

2. *What are the organization's strengths and weaknesses?* Visions are easier to fulfill if they can build on the school's strengths or avoid its weaknesses. For example, an analysis may show that the school has:

- strong relationships with parents and community
- a diminished tax base that threatens finances
- a rapidly changing population bringing more students who need individual attention, remedial work, and access to social services
- a capable, veteran staff that works hard to meet the needs of students
- a capable, veteran staff that is comfortable with the status quo
- aging buildings
- a cohesive written curriculum for all grade levels

As with teacher beliefs, these indicators may point toward a particular kind of vision or may affect the school's ability to carry out the vision. (Activity 5 in the previous chapter or Leithwood and Aitken's book offer several ways of looking at these issues.)

3. *Does the organization currently have a clearly stated vision? If so, what is it?* If a vision already exists, the leader's task changes; reviewing and renewing a vision requires a somewhat different approach than creating a vision for the first time.

However, the existence of a formal vision statement is no guarantee it plays a meaningful role in the school's culture. Do people accept it? Is it part of their everyday professional vocabulary? Do they judge their actions by their effect on the vision? Or do they give it only lip service? (For an aid in answering these questions, see Survey 2: Assessing the Vision.)

4. *What strategy is currently being followed to fulfill the current vision? Is it working?* Leithwood and colleagues (1994) say that useful visions provide guides to action by pointing out the discrepancies between what is and what ought to be. Just as physicians must understand the healthy body to make a diagnosis, educational leaders must base their decisions on a vision of the healthy school. A true strategy explicitly links these decisions to the vision.

The key questions here are:

- Has the school examined its current program in light of the vision?
- What *specific* actions are currently being taken as a response to the vision?
- What amount of this year's budget is being used for *direct* support of the vision?
- Is progress toward the vision formally assessed at least once a year?

Survey 2

ASSESSING THE VISION

Respond to each statement on a scale from 1 (= "strongly disagree") to 5 (="strongly agree").

1. This school has a clear educational vision for the future.

1————————2————————3————————4————————5

2. Most teachers in this school understand the vision.

1————————2————————3————————4————————5

3. Most teachers in this school support the vision.

1————————2————————3————————4————————5

4. This school has a strong sense of purpose; we know where we're headed.

1————————2————————3————————4————————5

5. People in this school frequently refer to the vision.

1————————2————————3————————4————————5

6. I fully support this school's philosophy of education.

1————————2————————3————————4————————5

7. The teaching that goes on in this school is consistent with the vision we've established.

1————————2————————3————————4————————5

8. The school regularly assesses the progress we're making toward the vision.

1————————2————————3————————4————————5

9. We're closer to the vision now than we were a year ago.

1————————2————————3————————4————————5

10. When teachers are hired, we look for someone whose philosophy is consistent with what we're trying to achieve here.

1————————2————————3————————4————————5

5. *If the organization stays on the current path, where will it be heading in the next decade? Is that good?* Here is where leaders must apply their future vision, trying to determine how the environment may change in coming years, and how the changes will affect the school. The use of the "What If...?" and Delphi methods described in chapter 2 (Activities 6 and 7) will be especially helpful at this point.

6. *Does the system—structures, processes, resources—support the current direction?* For example, if the vision calls for "technological literacy," does the budget provide sufficient technological resources? If the vision calls for a significant shift of direction, are teachers provided with appropriate training or the time to collaborate on necessary changes?

7. *Does the culture support reflection, experimentation, and collaboration?* Visions require teachers to submit their current practices to examination and align the real with the ideal through collaborative action. Not surprisingly, schools with a history of purposeful change find it easier to take on more change (Conley). Survey 3 in chapter 6 may be helpful in exploring these questions.

When Is a School Ready for Vision?

The short answer is simple: *now*. Schools should always be moving toward some image of a desired future. However, different situations may call for different strategies.

If teachers are accustomed to collaboration and share a common philosophy, the leader can move ahead by helping the staff express those beliefs in a written vision statement. (If a written statement already exists, the principal can focus on its reaffirmation and effective implementation.)

If, however, there is little evidence of faculty cohesion or instructional experimentation, then the principal may need to work on building readiness before launching a high-profile vision project. Louis and Miles found that the high schools they studied sometimes didn't arrive at a formal vision until they had done several years of diverse, small-scale experiments. These efforts identified emerging "themes" that could eventually coalesce into a true vision. This incremental strategy works only if the leader consciously seeks an answer to the question, "What are we working toward?" That is, what do these experiments tell us about our values, beliefs, and emerging vision?

Whatever the circumstances confronting the principal, the key is recognizing that vision is a process rather than an event. There is no preordained timetable or required format.

WHOSE VISION IS IT, ANYWAY?

With a careful assessment of the school's readiness, principals stand poised to make two strategic decisions that will determine the nature—and perhaps the success—of the vision:

- Will the vision be issued from the top down or grown from the bottom up?

- Who will participate in formulating and giving life to the vision?

TOP DOWN VS. BOTTOM UP

Does vision develop from the top down or from the bottom up? Is it the creation of a heroic, charismatic leader who articulates it and persuades others to go along, or does it bubble up from the shared dreams and values of everyone in the organization?

For most people, the term *vision* evokes images of dynamic, forceful leaders who paint vivid portraits of the future and stir people to action: Lee Iacocca, Bill Gates, Martin Luther King, Jr. Implicit in these images is the assumption that vision is the product of an individual mind that conceives it, voices it, and sells it to others.

However, current discussions seem to favor the idea of *shared* vision that grows from the collective aspirations of everyone in the organization. Peter Senge defines it this way:

> A vision is truly shared when you and I have a similar picture and are committed to one another having it, not just to each of us, individually, having it. When people truly share a vision they are connected, bound together by a common aspiration.

Proponents of this view argue that top-down vision is inadequate, even in the hands of a brilliant communicator. With broad involvement, the vision benefits from many different perspectives, and people who have seen their ideas come to life through an extended process of dialogue are much more likely to commit themselves enthusiastically.

The research literature offers no clear evidence on this point, and one can find thoughtful arguments on both sides of the issue. Conley leans toward shared vision but concedes that a top-down approach can work. Robert Fritz contends that a vision can be *shared* without being *coauthored* (everyone must help bring the vision to life, but not everyone need be involved in formulating it). He says that people who dismiss a vision because they didn't have input are more concerned with themselves than with the organization.

Bryan Smith takes a pragmatic view, suggesting that participation occupies a continuum determined by the organization's readiness. At one end, the leader operates by *telling*: it's the leader's vision and everyone is expected to fall in line. A less direct approach is *selling*, in which the leader has the vision but tries to win the employees' commitment. In *testing*, the leader has an idea but wants the group's reactions before proceeding. In *consulting*, the leader solicits ideas from the group and synthesizes them into a vision. Finally, leaders can opt for *cocreating*, in which visioning is a group process. Smith says organizations should be working toward cocreation, but may have to begin with more directiveness (Senge and colleagues).

Deciding which route to take is a matter of shrewd judgment, dependent on the leader's knowledge of the school, the community, and his or her own capabilities. Principals with a gift for eloquence will do better with a selling approach than will a leader with limited stage presence; those with patience and well-honed negotiating skills may gravitate toward shared vision. In some schools, teachers may gratefully accept confident, assertive leadership from the principal; in others, the first hint of a top-down mandate may serve as a call to arms.

The top-down approach offers certain advantages. For example, schools in a state of crisis may be receptive to a leader who maps out the future and says, "This is the way it will be." As David Hurst points out, when employees are bombarded with daily evidence that things just aren't working—when they can see the organization's failure in their own experience—they are more likely to listen to someone who says there is a better way.

Fresh starts may also be opportune moments for leaders to assert their personal vision. Principals who are new to a school don't carry the weight of long-established expectations, and teachers expect some change. Similarly, the opening of a new school is an occasion when staff members appreciate the sense of direction and coherence that a well-articulated vision can provide.

However, the top-down approach has some important limitations. For one thing, it requires an ability to phrase ideas clearly and persuasively, along with a personal style that inspires confidence. Not all leaders have the kind of charisma that can sweep people off their feet.

More importantly, the institution may not be in the market for what the leader is selling. This is often the case in "good" schools, where teachers are competent and committed, resources are adequate, and the community is satisfied. People who are content with the present have little motivation to go looking for the future. They may play along as long as the creator actively pushes, but when the visionary leaves, so does the vision.

Finally, no matter how well the vision is conceived and articulated, implementation will reveal inconsistencies, blind spots, and unforeseen problems. Unless the leader is prepared to share ownership by permitting modifications to the original vision, the mounting difficulties will lead to disenchantment (Conley).

Jean Wincek documented what can happen when an exciting vision is treated as the property of leaders. She observed the first year of a magnet school designed to provide a responsive student-oriented environment based on multiage "family" groupings. The vision was originally voiced by a school board member and lovingly developed by an enthusiastic director of staff development. The principal, for her part, bought into the vision and committed herself to keeping it intact.

The vision was stated broadly enough that the teachers—all well-respected veterans who had volunteered—accepted it without question as consistent with their beliefs. Eager to get on with the detailed planning, they declined to spend much time exploring their differing interpretations of the vision. When problems inevitably arose, attempts to voice concerns were treated by the principal as threats to the vision, and uncomfortable questions were not discussed. By the end of the first year, there was still no consensus on what the vision meant in practice, and the staff still was not operating as a cohesive group.

On the other side of the coin, developing shared vision is a much more complex and demanding process. Leaders must be able to discern a note of harmony in a multitude of voices and orchestrate it through the inevitable disagreements, confusions, and frustrations. Terry Deal and Kent Peterson note, "Every school is a repository of unconscious sentiments, expectations, and hopes that carry the code of the collective dream." The principal's job is to look beneath surface issues and events to find "the deeper dreams."

In addition, shared vision calls the principal to make a difficult sacrifice: letting go of parts of his or her personal vision (Conley and Goldman). Many school leaders have strong philosophical commitments and a passionate concern for children. Shared vision requires them to put aside any idea that they will remake the school in their own image. Instead, they must sort through their beliefs, distinguishing those that are peripheral ("how I would teach if I were still in the classroom") from those that are nonnegotiable ("how we *must* teach if our students are to succeed").

Despite the ambiguities, most writers on vision agree on two points:

- The leader is always actively involved; anything resembling a laissez-faire approach is doomed to failure.

- No matter who formulates the vision, it must ultimately become community property.

WHO SHOULD BE INVOLVED?

Assuming a principal decides to develop a jointly owned vision from the ground up, another issue surfaces: Who should participate? Should the entire faculty be involved, or will a representative group be able to do the job more efficiently? And should parents and other community members play an active role?

These questions create an unavoidable tension between inclusiveness and efficiency. On the one hand, gaining widespread commitment to the vision is more likely when all stakeholders have had a chance to participate. On the other hand, the larger the group, the clumsier the process.

Possible participants can be found in four main groups: teachers, parents, community members, and students.

Teachers. Teachers, who must ultimately enact the vision on a daily basis, are the most likely partners in the visioning process. Having entered teaching with considerable idealism, they often respond enthusiastically to the prospect of seeing those early dreams realized. At the same time, they bring a hard-nosed practicality to the process, demanding that the vision be workable in classroom terms. Where teachers are deeply involved in formulating the vision—and feel themselves to be true "owners"—it evolves into a *covenant*—a behavioral guide having moral force (Sergiovanni).

Parents. While most educators consider "parental involvement" to be a basic axiom, they also display considerable ambivalence about following through. Parents are wild cards: highly independent, not always objective about their children, and inconsistent in participation.

When parents are invited into the inner circle, the usual glossy public relations facade ("we're just one big happy family!") starts to crumble. Parents will see disagreements and bickering, they will get glimpses into the school's micropolitical arena, and they will catch teachers in unguarded moments. For that reason, teachers often resist deep parental involvement (Jo Blase and Joseph Blase 1997).

But there are persuasive reasons for including parents at a deep level. One is ethical. Seymour Sarason calls it the "political principle": those who are deeply affected by a decision have a right to be represented in making that decision.

Second, parents can contribute a perspective that no one else has. Teachers see students in a school environment for seven hours a day; parents see them in many other settings for much longer periods. They have "up-close and personal" perspectives on the way school is affecting (or not affecting) their children.

Third, the history of school reform is filled with stories of schools that set off to pursue a vision without bothering to involve the parents, only to run head-on into a brick wall. Parents, like much of the American public, tend to have rather conservative educational visions. Public Agenda, a nonpartisan research group, found that the vast majority of the citizens they interviewed were preoccupied with "safety, order, and the basics," and were ambivalent about new instructional approaches:

> The large majority of Americans are uncomfortable with many of these changes. Overall, the public seems to have a more traditional view of what should be happening in the classroom. They want to see students learning some of the same things—in the same ways—that they learned in school. (Jean Johnson and John Immerwahr)

Thus, what educators see as a state-of-the-art reform may appear to parents as the kind of risky New Age experiment to which they don't want their children subjected.

Finally, in today's superheated culture, seemingly innocent issues may become politicized at any time. Many school leaders who thought outcome-based education was just a straightforward means of assessment have been stunned to find it attacked as a government plot to subvert family values. When parents are involved from the ground up, conflicts are less likely to be fueled by rumors and misinformation.

Involving parents at a deep level—and making them vital contributing participants—increases the complexity of the vision process, but also enriches and fortifies the vision.

Community members. Educators often consider community members to be in the same class as parents, but even more remotely involved; those who don't have children in school are assumed to be preoccupied with lower tax rates. As with parents, educators are sometimes reluctant to invite "outsiders" into the decision-making process.

But David Mathews argues that there are moral and practical reasons for the public at large to be involved:

> The public schools are really the *public's* schools, and the public's involvement is not by sufferance of the educational authorities. Citizens belong in the school's hallways because they are *their* hallways.

Mathews says that twentieth-century education has become so professionalized that community members are no longer convinced that schools are serving *them*. Resentful at being talked down to or ignored, the public's relation to the schools is like a marriage in which the fire has gone out: convenient, for the time being, but no strong attachment.

Most administrators acknowledge that schools are creatures of society, and that many of the problems they struggle with originate elsewhere. Thus, it makes little sense to devise a vision whose field of view fails to extend beyond the school boundaries. Mathews says that the vision for education should originate in the purposes of the community and help bring the community as a whole closer to its dreams. Schools will be able to change only if they can bring the community along.

Blending this community purpose with the visions of the educators who must carry it out may be the most challenging part of the vision process. Chapter 4 considers this issue in greater depth.

Students. Students are the forgotten group in vision development. The reasons are understandable. Children and adolescents have less experience, less perspective, and less maturity than adults. As minors, they are not accorded the moral right to participation that adults are automatically given. As clients, their presence during policy deliberations can be threatening to teacher authority.

Yet students provide a piece of information that no one else can: how the school affects the thinking and emotions of the people it is designed to help. Students can often speak eloquently of their lives in school. At times their unvarnished feedback can be distressing or unsettling, but their candor is a vivid reminder of how much the vision is needed.

Clearly, the involvement of students in the vision process presents the principal with some delicate tactical questions, but the difficulties do not appear insurmountable. James Johnson argues that "the secret is effective communication." Principals must know what they want from student participation and make sure that students understand their role. Involvement can take many forms, from participation on committees to filling out questionnaires. (See Leithwood and Aitken for a sample student survey.) For those concerned that student participation might infringe on teacher power, Johnson points out that students already possess the ultimate power: whether or not to learn.

BUILDING A STRUCTURE FOR INVOLVEMENT

However inclusive the process will be, principals must provide appropriate structures for supporting involvement. One of the greatest enemies of reform is confusion about new roles: Who is responsible for doing what? M. Peg Lonnquist and Jean King describe an ambitious "cutting-edge" middle school that was launched with high hopes and much rhetoric. Four experienced, highly capable teachers were given leadership roles but without anyone determining what those roles encompassed. The result, in the words of another teacher, was confusion:

> They're called the leadership team, and they're supposed to lead, but there's a lot of ambiguity as to what they are leading, and why and where. In three years no one's given a clear answer to me, so it's clear as mud to new staff.

Not only did the vision falter, but the school climate turned rancorous and hostile.

The exact form of involvement structures will depend on the individual circumstances of each school, but several guiding principles apply to most situations.

1. *Not everyone needs to be involved in the same way or to the same degree.* Typically, a number of stakeholders are enthused; others are skeptical; some are indifferent; and everyone is busy. Ideally, there should be avenues through which every stakeholder can participate as much as desired. The menu can include such things as discussions at faculty meetings, written surveys, informational meetings, and task-oriented committees. Two types of groups deserve special mention: steering committees and focus groups.

A core group serving as a steering committee can provide unity and cohesion to the process by addressing the inevitable difficulties and misunderstandings that will arise (Dolan). Does the principal have an accurate perception of teachers' attitudes toward the vision? Do some people feel left out of the process? Do other people feel overburdened or confused? The steering council is a place where such questions can be discussed honestly.

From time to time, focus groups can sharpen insights into the change process (Tony Wagner). Focus groups consist of 10-15 people led by a facilitator discussing a structured set of questions. For example, if the core group in its deliberations has identified three priorities for the school, the focus groups could be asked questions such as:

• Do you also see these as key priorities?

- Are there other priorities the council has overlooked?

- If we accept these as priorities, what kinds of actions would you see as appropriate?

Such meetings not only offer opportunities for others to participate, they provide valuable feedback for the steering committee, which can then shape its work accordingly. Because the focus groups are small, and the agenda is structured, there is an opportunity for meaningful discussion and reflection.

2. *Keep information flowing between the core and the periphery.* Core groups of enthusiasts are mixed blessings. They provide much of the human energy and positive thinking that vitalize the vision, but they sometimes divide the school into in-groups and out-groups.

Core meetings can become intellectual hot-houses in which participants feed on each other's ideas, to the point where they start considering radical proposals that aren't on anybody else's radar screen (a tendency that is strengthened by the fact that core groups tend to attract those who are excited at the prospect of change). Principals must find ways to keep the core in touch with the perceptions and attitudes of those who are less actively involved.

At the same time, those on the periphery must know how the vision is progressing. A sense of openness is vital. Meetings of the steering committee should be publicly posted with agendas available in advance. Meeting summaries should be promptly distributed to all interested parties, and the principal should routinely keep stakeholders up to date on progress and alert them when sensitive issues are being discussed.

3. *Be flexible about determining representation.* If people are to take the vision process seriously, they must feel that their views are represented in the deliberations. However, formalizing the representation process may be counterproductive.

For one thing, when people become focused on representation and voting, they tend to shift into a political, self-defensive mode. Vision development does better with dialogue and consensus than with debate and voting. In addition, formal representation does not always get the right people into the right roles (for example, the union may send someone whose main concern is protecting the contract rather than transforming the school).

In certain cases, formal representation may be a prudent tactic, particularly if the community or faculty is so factionalized that informal choices would be viewed with suspicion. But principals will often get better results by recruiting participants or asking for volunteers. In doing this recruiting, however, they must remain conscious of key factions and constituencies in the school community.

THE LEADER'S STRATEGY

The literature on school change is complex and sometimes ambiguous, but it seems to agree on one central premise: the principal is the catalyst, even when the school is moving toward shared governance and collective vision. The final set of strategic considerations revolves around the principal.

The principal's philosophy and style will influence his or her strategic choices. Principals without a strong personal vision will make little headway with a top-down approach. Those who are committed to parental and community involvement will seek to develop an inclusive vision process. Those with an assertive approach and good selling skills may find it easier to use a "take charge" strategy.

In addition, the principal's history with the school will also be significant. Consider the following scenarios.

Scenario 1: The principal has been in this school for a number of years. Leaders in this situation have the advantage of knowing their staff, district, and community; they are likely to know where the land mines are buried, and can proceed with proper caution. On the other hand, the mutual history can inhibit change: by this time, everyone has formed expectations about the principal and has adjusted their behavior accordingly. If the principal suddenly veers in a new direction, initiating new goals or adopting a new leadership style, teachers are likely to feel confused and perhaps even betrayed (James Conway and Frank Calzi).

In this scenario, two approaches will be helpful. First, principals can watch for everyday opportunities to point a new direction. For example, if the faculty is debating the discipline issue (for the tenth time), the principal can use the discussion to raise some deeper issues. What kind of behavior do we expect? What help do we give students to get there? What kind of help *could* we give? If the behavior isn't reaching expectations, why not? Steering the discussion in this direction may, in a small way, generate new visions. And even though discipline will never constitute a complete vision of the future, exploring the issue can provide a valuable foundation for easing into more comprehensive discussions.

Second, if the principal does decide to take the school in bold new directions, it's best to prepare the faculty by explaining what has led up to the decision, what changes they can expect from the principal, and what changes will be required of them. If teachers understand the rationale, they will find it easier to adapt to the changes (rather than wondering if the principal is having some kind of midlife crisis).

Scenario 2: The principal is new to the school, which has no apparent collective vision. Here the dynamics are very different. On the one hand, the principal doesn't know the school (and perhaps not the district or community). How ready is the school for change? Who are the existing leaders on the staff? What individual visions of excellence currently drive the teachers? Where are the sacred cows? The new principal has scant evidence to answer those questions.

On the other hand, there is opportunity here as well. The new principal doesn't carry the weight of established expectations; most teachers recognize this blank slate and are usually anxious to know what the new agenda will be. Often there is a honeymoon period in which the staff, recognizing the principal's need to make a mark, will good-naturedly accept some new initiatives.

This grace period offers an opening for quick decisive action that sets the tone and establishes momentum. It also offers plentiful opportunities for missteps. The key is how teachers perceive the school. If they see it as floundering, disorganized, or chaotic, assertive behavior may inspire confidence that the leader has a direction. If, on the other hand, they are generally pleased with the state of affairs, quick action may be resented as an outsider's attack on their dedication or competence. (Even in schools where there is no collective vision, teachers may cultivate *individual* visions of excellence and be justly proud of them.)

It may be possible to signal a new order without setting the final destination prematurely. One new leader offered to meet individually with all faculty members to chat about whatever was on their minds. This put him in a listening mode, but also implied that changes might be on the horizon. Blase and Blase (1997) quote a middle school principal whose bubbly approach seemed to strike a balance between assertiveness and receptivity:

> I just walked down the hall and asked people, "Do you have a *vision?*" One person said, "When I'm drinking, sometimes I get one." One guy told me he hadn't had one since he was in college in the 60s. I said, "Hang on. I'm serious. Do you have a belief? Can you tell me why you're here?" People said, "Boy, I don't think so." But we need to have a vision! I told the faculty that I'm burning up to do something for these kids, and I'm fired up to do something for the [teaching] folks! So everybody wrote out his or her vision for the school, and we took those little paper bricks and built a foundation.

Scenario 3: The principal is new to the school, which has a clear collective vision that is actively supported by the faculty. This scenario may be the most challenging, for three reasons.

First, the normal process of gaining acceptance and credibility is complicated by the fact that the existing vision makes the school's culture much more closely knit than usual. The new leader is likely to be seen as an outsider who will be judged on his or her willingness to support the current direction. One teacher gave a glimpse of the challenge facing the new principal:

> Somebody new coming in—I think it would be very, very difficult for anybody to come into this school and try to lead a bunch of people who already have a notion of what they want to do and where they want to go. But you can't replace [former principal]. I don't care who it is. [New principal] is wonderful but [former principal] is a visionary leader. (Marlene Johnson)

Second, the leader's task here is different. The existence of a healthy vision shifts the focus to implementation rather than creation. Rather than being the innovators and creators of the vision, new principals must become guardians of the vision. They may have to put aside some cherished personal views and play the role of "step-parent."

Third, the existence of a vision does not mean that all is well. There may be great enthusiasm and considerable rhetoric, but beneath the surface problems may be brewing. Margaret Cohen and Loyal Packer studied a school in which the new principal found a recently formulated vision firmly supported by a "zealous" teacher steering committee. Yet further investigation showed that other teachers were confused and conflicted about the vision. The principal took a cautious approach, communicating his willingness to be flexible and asking "Where do I fit in?" At the same time, he gradually began expressing his support for the vision and telling people, in effect, "This is a winning program. We're staying in it, and if you can't join us, I'll help you transfer."

Like so many other educational decisions, choosing a vision strategy is a matter of "practical wisdom"—a combination of reflection, intuition, and hope. There is no way to determine the right choice with complete certainty, but the saving grace is that there is evidently more than one way of doing it right. The next chapter looks at several very different paths that schools have followed to launch their vision.

FOUR

PATHWAYS TO VISION

A business consultant tells how he once attempted to shake up a group of high-level executives by giving them a task beyond their expertise: cooking. He's never forgotten the image of one frustrated leader standing helplessly, an egg in each hand, saying, "Separate eggs? From *what?*"

Developing a shared vision plunges school leaders into a similar situation. For all their experience and talents, they've never done it before. And the recipes don't always help.

Consider the standard advice for formulating a vision statement: choose a representative group of educators, parents, and citizens; convene a series of meetings; and decide on a vision. That last step, of course, is the catch. Exactly *how* can a diverse group of individuals wrap their minds around such a broad task and reach something resembling consensus?

What often happens, of course, is that the group becomes indiscriminate, accepting all suggestions to avoid conflict, or it conducts the discussion on a high level of abstraction, dealing with glittering generalities that might mean anything—or nothing.

To draw the common vision from a representative group of stakeholders is a leadership act of the first order. It requires patience, diplomacy, and, above all, a deep capacity for dialogue.

As it happens, however, schools do not always get to their vision in such a direct fashion. Researchers have consistently found that vision *evolves* over time, and that there is no single pathway (Conley and colleagues; Louis and Miles; Blase and Blase 1997). Thus the first section of this chapter examines the experience of several schools whose visions did not come from a carefully orchestrated plan. The second section provides some guidelines for principals who wish to lead their schools through a more systematic process.

Evolving Toward Vision

In the press of daily events—the phone calls, the mandates, the emergencies—school leaders sometimes feel like they're riding a small boat on a raging river. Just staying afloat is a victory; taking control of the boat and steering it to a precise location three miles downstream are much harder. Yet some principals are able to do this, not by overpowering the river and moving in a straight line to the goal, but by maneuvering through the white water and the eddies, shooting ahead where they can, patiently paddling when they must, and continually edging closer to the goal.

Imposed Vision

Even in an age of site-based management, schools are seldom fully autonomous. There is always a district context that asserts its influence on a school's vision. Schools are usually given a fair amount of latitude, but sometimes the board or central office wants to move in a particular direction.

This kind of imposed vision is troublesome for principals, since it may not be a good fit for their school. In some cases, the mandate is driven by politics, as the central administration seeks to satisfy some constituency or just give a state-of-the-art gloss to the publicity machine. Those pushing the vision may be more interested in *having* the vision than in any particular effect it has on the school. But even when the central-office staff is deeply committed and ready to offer substantive support, it is still the school site where it must be worked out.

Not surprisingly, success under such circumstances depends on the principal's ability to mediate between what the district wants and what the school can accept. Chenoweth and Kushman studied a district in which the central office was promoting Henry Levin's "accelerated-schools" concept. (Because this approach requires a comprehensive rethinking of the way that teachers work together, it has many of the characteristics of a vision.)

Three principals accepted the challenge. (It isn't clear how free their choice was. Presumably, they could have chosen not to accept, but it's possible that political calculations played a role as well.) All three principals found things in the idea that they liked, but two of them seemed to be less cognizant of what was involved or what it required. The third was enthused because it came close to her own philosophy.

Not surprisingly, the enthusiastic principal had better success in persuading teachers to adopt the program. Chenoweth and Kushman observe:

> It appears to be most critical for the principal to be actively involved, modeling the process, and sending strong signals of being knowledgeable, confident, and possessing a "can do" attitude.

However, more than enthusiasm was involved. The other two principals took a direct approach in attempting to persuade faculty, bringing in speakers to explain the program and outline its advantages. The other principal worked more indirectly, relying not on logical arguments but on helping teachers see how the new idea was consistent with what they were already doing and how it might help them do things even better. She also made sure teachers had a chance to visit other schools where the idea was being successfully used. Seeing the idea in action gave concrete reality to an idea that was inherently ambiguous. The authors note that no one can sell an idea better than teachers who are using it.

Another perspective on imposed vision comes from Wincek's study of a new magnet school whose vision originated with a school board member and was enthusiastically supported by a central-office administrator. Despite faculty and staff's expressed agreement and enthusiasm about the vision, they experienced a difficult first year.

Wincek places the blame on too little communication and dialogue. The teachers, assuming that everyone shared their particular interpretation of the vision, had been eager to get down to the nuts and bolts of implementation. The principal, eager to do well on her first assignment, took the role of "guardian of the vision." In trying to protect it, she sent subtle signals that criticism of the vision was not appreciated, leaving problems to simmer beneath the surface rather than being openly discussed.

The lesson in both these cases is not that imposed vision cannot work, but that it must be allowed to "breathe." *Any* vision will deviate from the original pristine version as it collides with reality. Even if fundamentally sound, it must be adapted to the needs and conditions of a particular institution. The existence of a prefabricated vision, combined with pressure from above, may short-circuit the lengthy dialogue that is needed. Chenoweth and Kushman emphasize the importance of the "courtship" period, in which leaders try to develop a critical mass of support for the vision:

> Reformers who ignore the meaning of change from the various stakeholder perspectives do so at their own peril, because concerns, issues, and differing points of view left unaddressed in the early stages can result in a loss of commitment and even sabotage in later stages.

GROPING TOWARD A VISION

In some cases, principals begin the search for vision with no clear plan or formalized procedures. Driven by the conviction that the school needs to move ahead, they start thinking aloud about where it should be headed.

Marlene Johnson describes a school in which teachers gradually came to the realization that the existing curriculum wasn't working for their students. At that point there was no coherent vision, just a gut-level feeling that there had to be a better way. Over the next few years, the school embraced a distinctive vision centered on Henry Levin's accelerated-schools program, resulting in improved student performance and national recognition.

How did it happen? There was no grand plan, just concerned teachers and an enterprising principal who recognized an opportunity. One teacher said,

> I think Henry Levin came across her desk by accident. You know, and it just happened to come at the right time. And we all knew we were floundering. Everybody here in the building knew we were not being successful... so we were ready. And she could see that. Like ripe fruit.

But this was not the kind of ripe fruit that falls into one's lap. The principal spent that first year engaging in energetic, nonstop dialogue with the faculty. She characterized it as "Socratic" dialogue, laced with questions like "Why?" "Why not?" "Where is it written?"

and "What do you think?" She impressed the faculty with her willingness to admit ignorance and to trust in their perceptions.

This energetic questioning was accompanied by other actions, both substantive and symbolic, that created an aura of change. She made sure the building was in top shape for the first day, helped teachers put up bulletin boards, invited school board members to observe, and transformed routine faculty meetings into professional development seminars. Finally, as the vision began to take shape, she worked with teachers who were not ready to accept it and began to nudge a few of them into transfers.

In succeeding years, the principal's contributions included bringing parents into the building, sharing relevant research with teachers, explaining the school to the outside community, and finding resources to support the vision.

What this example suggests is that amidst the turmoil and distractions of daily school life, opportunistic principals can find openings for vision to shine through. The case described by Johnson suggests several guiding principles.

1. The fuel for the vision came from teachers' grappling with a problem that was very real and very close to their identities as teachers. Knowing in their hearts that they were not helping their students succeed, they were receptive to promising new approaches. Without this motivation, the accelerated-schools concept, no matter how plausible and well supported by research, would have been just another idea to be discussed and forgotten.

2. The principal did not treat the issue as an occasion for technical problem-solving or quick fixes. Instead, she used it as a wedge to open up more fundamental questions. Why are we dissatisfied? What kind of student success would make us happy? What would we have to do to get where we want to go? This kind of questioning not only drove teachers to think more deeply about the issues, it pushed them into thinking of possibilities that went beyond existing practice.

3. Developing the vision was clearly a shared process. All indications are that the principal did not take over the school intending to implement an accelerated-schools program. Whatever her initial vision—Johnson is not sure she ever articulated it to anyone—she was willing to support the collective dream that developed among the faculty. From the beginning, it was everyone's vision.

4. Through her actions, the principal demonstrated unwavering commitment to the idea that it was not only possible to have a vision but to bring it into being. Because of her energy, it was difficult for teachers not to believe that good things would happen.

Undoubtedly, the process at this school benefitted from some special circumstances. Even before the principal arrived, the teachers were conscious of their dissatisfaction with the status quo and willing to talk about it (something that isn't true in all schools). The fact that the principal was new probably made a difference. As with any new principal, teachers were a bit off balance; she hit the ground running and never gave the status quo a chance. Finally, the school had a low profile in the district; it was not considered a showcase school, so higher level administrators were willing to let it go its own way.

Yet the principal's key strategies in this case would undoubtedly be useful in many contexts. The lessons here seem to be:

- Build on teacher concerns.
- Keep asking, "Where are we trying to go?"
- Share ownership.
- Keep pushing.

CONTINUAL EVOLUTION

In the schools we've been discussing, vision follows no particular timetables. No one event stands out as the starting point, nor is there any point at which participants stop and say, "We're there." There is just a gradually dawning realization that *something* is happening and that the school is moving toward a better way of working.

Some schools are able to maintain this sense of momentum over decades. Victoria Boyd and Shirley Hord studied a school whose vision could be traced back almost twenty years through four different principals. It began when a new principal was brought in with the mandate to develop a distinctive program that could save a school with declining enrollment. She developed a highly child-centered approach designed to create a "family" feeling throughout the school. Succeeding principals honored that vision but added new elements such as an emphasis on teacher development and academic proficiency. After two decades of development, teachers had a strong sense of "the way we do things around here," yet had not let up in their commitment to finding even better ways of doing things.

This example suggests that vision is not an event—a onetime shift from old paradigm to new paradigm—but a continual movement toward an ever-changing target. Schools of this sort become *learning organizations* (see chapter 6).

PRAGMATIC VISIONARIES

From the above examples, it's clear that vision is not always a grand crusade accompanied by banners and trumpets. Sometimes the process seems to have accidental beginnings, as external pressures or internal crises nudge a school out of the status quo. Often the principal is not out front waving a flag, but working quietly in the background.

Laraine Hong, describing a reform effort in an elementary school, explained the principal's approach this way:

> Anne was on a personal mission. She wasn't delivering speeches or sending out memoranda listing dozens of objectives. Instead, she was starting at the edges—in informal conversations, the agenda topics for staff meetings, how teacher evaluations were to be conducted, her daily wanderings through classrooms, Principal's Awards for positive student behavior, articles on instruction attached to our weekly bulletins, and complimentary notes and comments to teachers and staff.

This school did develop a formal vision statement (as part of a grant application); significantly, however, that effort resulted from an impromptu lounge conversation between the principal and two teachers.

The lesson to be learned from all these cases seems to be twofold.

1. *Developing a vision does not necessarily begin with a formal, highly publicized statement.* It *does* begin with a leader who relentlessly seeks to keep the school moving forward—often in small ways—whenever opportunity knocks. Such leaders seem to be guided by a deep sense of personal values; however, they do not always package these as an explicit vision, and they remain open to the ideas of others.

2. *Developing a vision is not a neat linear process with clear beginnings and steady progress toward the goal.* There are times to steam ahead, times to back off, and times to take a detour. As Hong says of her principal, "Anne had to know when to suggest, when to nudge, when to wait. She had to be assertive enough to push us a few steps forward, but indirect and patient enough to let us find our own way." In short, visionary principals seem to have the passion of revolutionaries, but the patient pragmatism of moderates.

Building Vision from the Ground Up

If some schools seem to evolve their way to vision, others use a frontal assault. In recent years, many schools have consciously set out to *create* a vision. Typically, they go through an extended dialogue that leads to a written vision statement, which is then used as a blueprint to guide the change process.

The remainder of this chapter examines the challenges of a direct approach to vision, looking first at the special kind of dialogue required for a successful vision statement, and then suggesting some ways of beginning the discussion.

Understanding the Challenge of Deliberation

Convening a meeting of typical citizens and asking "What should the schools be doing?" is a little like walking into a sports bar and asking "Who was the greatest baseball player of all time?" The resulting discussion will stir passions, raise voices, and spark conflicts—all the more so because there is no objective way to determine the right answer.

Whatever their reservations about today's schools, people continue to care deeply about education. Americans take it for granted that the quality of a child's education will determine the quality of his or her life. They also assume that future society will be shaped by the kind of experiences children have in school. With so much at stake, discussions of educational purpose are always emotionally charged.

Unfortunately, most people (including educators) don't have appropriate models for this kind of discussion. When citizens meet over a complex or controversial issue, the typical result is either highly expressive behavior, with much venting of emotions, or defensive debating in which the goal is to forcefully assert one's own position to negate the other person's point of view.

Daniel Yankelovich says the problem is aggravated when the meeting has been convened by public officials who regard themselves as experts and who do not fully trust the public's judgment on complex issues. Too often the unspoken attitude is "We're the professionals who should know better."

David Mathews adds that public forums controlled by school leaders too often turn into PR exercises. "It is assumed that the public can be rallied through the standard means of publicity and marketing: the buyers are out there waiting to be told the benefits of the product." Citizens sense the attitude and either withdraw from participation or resent the officials.

However, both Mathews and Yankelovich, citing long experience with public-affairs forums, argue that the public is quite capable of engaging in thoughtful deliberation that leads to a measured judgment. Not everyone will be in complete agreement, of course, but there will be understanding and even respect for the differences. The deliberative approach described in the next section assumes a small-group discussion involving members of the public; however, it also applies to discussions among educators.

Creating a Dialogue

To create some kind of consensus out of the crazyquilt of public opinion, school leaders must establish a safe haven where a *dialogue* can occur. A dialogue is a conversation that seeks to form a judgment based on mutual understanding rather than aggressive debate. People still seek to persuade each other, but with the assumption that disagreement will lead to mutual learning and a more informed decision. Yankelovich describes it this way:

> In debate I present my unique way of looking at an issue, but—this is the key point—before forming a judgment I also take *your* way of looking at it into account. My point of view is enriched by my ability to incorporate your perspective. Together we seek to persuade each other and to arrive at a communal outlook which we call a judgment.

According to William Isaacs, effective dialogue progresses through a series of stages, from polite conversation to a communion that goes beyond mere words. The initial stage is recognizing and confronting disagreements. Most groups respond to conflict by politely ignoring it or by trying to resolve it on the spot. For purposes of dialogue, says Isaacs, it's much more important to ask, "Where does this disagreement come from?" That is, what different experiences have led the participants to their opposing positions? (Senge and colleagues).

Beyond the first stage, things become more difficult: progress appears to be slow and frustration mounts. But with the proper guidance, says Isaacs, this frustration can force people to look deeper into their own sometimes inconsistent beliefs. Eventually the conversation starts to flow more smoothly, and new insights emerge.

Most people, including school leaders, have relatively little experience with dialogue, so it can seem a painfully slow and inefficient process. To make it work, participants must share an understanding of the ground rules:

1. *Sincere respect for others' views.* This kind of respect is not just a matter of politeness—it grows from the sincere belief that others have valid contributions to make. Dialogue is not an exercise in managing opinion or making people feel good through participation.

This is often difficult for school leaders, because their professional knowledge and experience give them a more sophisticated understanding of the issues. However, deliberation about vision is focused more on ends than means; it does not require great technical expertise to voice one's beliefs about what students should gain from attending school. Similarly, a simplistic statement does not automatically invalidate the values that motivate it.

Another barrier is that previous experience has convinced some principals that public opinion is uninformed, erratic, and volatile—something that can turn on them at any time without warning. Yankelovich agrees that this is often true, but only because people have not been accorded an opportunity to arrive at a thoughtful judgment.

2. *Deep listening.* Isaacs recommends "listening behind the words," responding not just to the surface comments but the unstated feelings. George Manning and colleagues point out that thinking is about four times as fast as speaking, which means there is time to spare when listening to someone (which most people use to prepare their own arguments). But the lag time can be put to better use by

mentally summarizing the speaker's position so far; monitoring body language to sense the feelings behind the words; and asking why the person feels this way.

3. *Self-examination.* When people find themselves being annoyed or angered, they should ask why this is happening. Sometimes emotional reactions reveal one's own underlying assumptions—some of which may be beyond conscious recognition.

4. *Emphasis on consensus.* The most common mechanism for democratic decision-making is voting, which tends to be fair and efficient. However, voting also has some disadvantages:

- Participants may spend the discussion time counting heads rather than listening to viewpoints.

- Voting may lead to premature foreclosure; when participants face disagreement, they may be tempted just to vote and move on, rather than exploring the issues in depth.

- Voting creates winners and losers; even when done fairly, the minority may feel as though their voices have been silenced.

One alternative is *consensus*, which aims at getting everyone's consent to the decision. As John Gastil points out, this does not mean that everyone will completely agree, but they will achieve a reasonable level of acceptance (perhaps reflected in the phrase, "We'll agree to disagree").

The effort to secure each person's consent ensures that minority viewpoints will get a full hearing and improves the quality of listening that goes on in the group. Sometimes further discussion reveals that the conflict is not that serious and can be resolved by rephrasing the issue or making minor amendments. Even when that isn't possible, those in the minority tend to feel better because their views at least have been taken seriously.

Gastil notes that consensus is not flawless. It takes much more time than voting, and it requires participants who are willing to speak their minds even when they stand alone. While unanimous consent sounds highly idealistic, it has proved itself in the rough-and-tumble world of administration. Principals using shared decision-making often report that the faculty is able to negotiate satisfactory decisions without the use of voting (Blase and Blase 1997).

The Setting Is Important

High-quality dialogue is difficult to attain under the best of circumstances. Unfortunately, many school committees work in conditions far from ideal: sitting on uncomfortable chairs in an acoustically challenged cafeteria, sipping weak coffee, and always keeping one impatient eye on the clock.

Some schools, following the lead of businesses, begin the process with an intensive workshop or retreat that permits unbroken concentration on the task at hand. When the Bartholomew Consolidated School Corporation (Columbus, Indiana) brought its administrators together to develop a district mission, they met out of town for two days, including an overnight stay. That decision helped the group stay focused, says the district's assistant superintendent for curriculum and instruction, Linda DeClue. Since it was August, and everyone was thinking about the start of school, it was important not to be diverted. In addition, the district brought in an outside facilitator with a business background, something that added perspective and marked the session as more than just another meeting.

The Leader's Role in Deliberation

Deliberative groups require a skillful facilitator—ideally an outsider. Group members, including principals, can serve in that role, but there are significant disadvantages. First, anyone with a major stake in the vision will probably not be viewed as completely neutral, no matter how fair he or she attempts to be.

Second, when leaders facilitate, subordinates may perceive them as being "in charge" and defer to their perceived wishes. Finally, facilitators must devote most of their attention to *process*, making it difficult for them to engage fully with the ideas being presented.

When leaders serve as facilitator, they should make it clear which "hat" they are wearing at different points in the discussion. At times they will be acting as leader; at other times, they will be just another participant (Thomas Keyser).

Even when not acting as formal facilitators, principals will probably stand out in the crowd; participants will never completely forget that when the meeting ends, this is the person still in charge of the school. Thus, leaders will be watched carefully, and they can set the tone by the way they model the dialogue process. This can be done most effectively by suspending judgment on the validity of others' ideas and choosing language that emphasizes inquiry and understanding rather than debate.

ON THE LAUNCHPAD

Where does one start? The word "vision" can be intimidating; it seems to imply something so momentous, so dazzling, and so futuristic that it's hard to imagine creating one. Typically, the beginning will be characterized by hesitation, discomfort, and long silences. This is normal and even healthy; silence often leads to reflective thinking and surprising insights. Too much structure, or too much impatience to rush to the final grand vision, may prevent spontaneity and creativity.

However, it may help to have a few starting points that can serve as icebreakers. The activities listed below are designed for small groups (eight to fifteen participants) that will allow one to two hours for discussion. The activities themselves do not determine what the vision should be; they only stimulate thinking on the kinds of issues that are addressed by visions.

1. *Identifying Core Values.* Sergiovanni emphasizes the importance of schools being clear on core values—the ones they will protect at all costs. Such values become the standard for judging all decisions and actions, and will be a major influence on the vision.

The facilitator might begin by asking participants to think about what the school should stand for as it goes about its daily business. These might include values such as:

- recognizing and honoring human effort and achievement
- celebrating diversity
- practicing unconditional respect for others
- putting the welfare of children first
- empowering all members of the school community

If the group reaches consensus on several values, it can begin to test them against the current reality. What parts of our program best exemplify these values? In what ways do we fall short? Would an outside observer recognize from our actions that these were our values? Would our own people? The answers to those questions will point toward some obvious future directions.

2. *Prioritizing objectives.* In developing their visions, many schools start by identifying the educational objectives they most want to accomplish. Often they end up with dauntingly long—and ultimately meaningless—lists, simply because they aren't willing to deal with disagreements. Something more interesting happens when participants are limited to a small number of objectives; for example, what are the top seven objectives that should be at the center of the program? If the group is asked to achieve consensus, people are forced to defend their choices and examine their assumptions.

The resulting list of essential objectives does not constitute a mission, much less a vision, but it does offer clues. What themes are present? Which are the aims we feel most passionate about? How well are we currently achieving these aims? How do we know? (See figure 1 for a list of possible goals.)

3. *Graduation day, 2010.* In this activity, participants are asked to imagine this year's kindergarten class as they walk across the stage for their high school graduation twelve years hence. What has happened to these students? What are they like? What do they know,

Figure 1

PRIORITIZING EDUCATIONAL GOALS

Listed below are the knowledge, skills, and attitudes commonly given as desirable outcomes of public schooling. Thoughtful dialogue results when participants in a group are asked to achieve consensus (unanimous agreement) on which seven goals are most important. The guiding question for the discussion is "If we could be guaranteed of reaching just seven goals for all our students, which goals would we choose?"

- fluency in reading

- ability to communicate clearly in writing

- creativity

- skill in basic arithmetic computation

- understanding of math principles
- knowledge of key historical events
- knowledge of key scientific terms
- appreciation of great literature
- appreciation of great music
- appreciation of great art
- technological literacy
- accuracy in spelling
- sound moral values
- marketable skills
- high self-esteem
- understanding of basic scientific principles
- knowledge of basic principles of health and nutrition
- clear-cut vocational direction
- extensive vocabulary
- good manners
- ability to cooperate with others
- acceptance of others who are different
- knowledge of geography
- good citizenship
- fine arts skills
- self-discipline
- good penmanship
- ability to solve real-life problems
- critical thinking ability
- global awareness
- ability to form healthy relationships
- love of learning
- other_____

and what are they able to do? What values do they have? Where are they headed? How has the school achieved these results?

4. *The Impossible Dream.* (This is an adaptation of an activity suggested by John Hoyle.) In this activity, group members think of one or two "impossible" goals—things they would love to do or to have happen in the school that are considered unrealistic. As these ideas are shared with the group, they are written on a board or flip chart. Then each one is addressed with the question "What would it take to make this impossible dream possible?"

5. *Awards Day, 2000.* Hoyle suggests having participants imagine the school receiving a national award for innovation within the next decade. What would you want that award to be for? What would it take for that award to be accomplished?

6. *Where We Stand.* Survey 1: Assessing Teacher Beliefs, in the previous chapter, can serve as the jumping-off point for a dialogue on beliefs about teaching and learning. The survey may identify areas of conflict or consensus that can then be explored in greater depth. Are the conflicts true disagreements or just different emphases? Is there a way of reframing the issue so the conflict is reduced? For those areas in which there is consensus, how well are we practicing what we preach? Where are we successfully living out these beliefs, and where do we fall short? Overall, what does the pattern of responses suggest about a vision for this school?

7. *Mapping.* Many teachers approach the prospect of reform with strong attitudes that have been shaped by their previous experiences with change efforts. To help participants understand how those past experiences influence their current thinking, Mary Amsler and Kayla Kirsch of the Far West Educational Laboratory use an activity that asks teachers to "map" the history of change efforts at their school. Participants are given crayons and long pieces of paper and asked to respond with a visual answer to the question "How has our school gotten to where we are now?" The resulting drawings help explain the school's history with change and also provide insights into why change works—or doesn't.

It is important to emphasize again that these activities are just starting points. The real work of developing the vision will go on in the dialogue that takes place.

ENERGIZING THE PROCESS

At this point, the leader faces the most challenging part of the process: enlisting members of the school community in the dialogue and keeping the discussion going.

Involving Everyone

The kind of dialogue needed in developing a vision works best in a small-group setting, which implies that a core group or steering committee will do most of the work. However, as noted in chapter 3, it is also important to maintain close links between the core and the rest of the school community. Communication must be thorough and continual.

At a minimum, minutes, agendas, and reports should be freely distributed so that all stakeholders know what is happening with the vision. Perhaps even more important, the steering committee should actively solicit feedback from others. This can be done through surveys, discussions at faculty meetings, and even hallway conversations.

At times the committee may want to spin off task groups to study specific issues that come up or perhaps visit another school to see how it is implementing a particular program. In other cases, the steering group may want to replicate its own activities with a wider audience. For example, if the committee has spent some time prioritizing educational objectives, it might schedule a public forum that would take participants through the same activity, and then compare results.

This kind of involvement does two things. First, it broadens the participation base and allows other stakeholders to play a meaningful role. Second, it keeps the committee from getting too far out in front and helps them shape a vision that will be widely acceptable.

Providing Inspiration

The initial discussions are likely to be tentative and meandering, with participants looking nervously at one another and wondering how honest they can afford to be. At the end, if all goes well, the school will see the birth of a vibrant, motivating vision. In between is an ambiguous period in which participants move from skepticism to hope, from the attitude of "just another meeting" to genuine excitement. How this happens often seems mysterious, even to the partici-pants, but a number of observers have identified very concrete leadership behaviors that will help.

1. *Creating a Sense of Urgency.* John Kotter says that major reform efforts often fail because people simply don't accept the need for change. Denial is too easy, especially if there is no overt crisis, or if employees lack (or ignore) objective feedback about the organization's performance.

According to surveys by Public Agenda, 86 percent of teachers believe their own schools do a good or excellent job (Steve Farkas and Jean Johnson). Teachers do recognize problems, but they tend to put the blame on external factors, such as lack of financing and growing social problems. As one teacher said, "The school system isn't bro-ken. Society is broken."

Such perceptions, combined with traditional skepticism about the value of large-scale reform, mean that many teachers will be blasé about the need for a vision. How can leaders break through these attitudes to spark genuine interest?

Kotter, speaking to a business audience, recommends creating a crisis, such as allowing a big enough financial loss to get everyone's attention. School leaders, operating in a very public arena, may need to search for lower risk strategies. One alternative is providing everyone with unvarnished objective information about the school's performance, especially if the trend lines are down. Surveys of student or community attitudes can also be revealing.

Creating urgency requires a deft touch, since principals are usually expected to buffer their staff from criticism. Too heavy an emphasis on the negative may be interpreted by teachers as an attack on their competence or dedication. The ideal message will convey the idea that "we're doing well under the circumstances... but it's time to change the circumstances."

2. *Empowering People To Voice Their Dreams.* Many teachers learn to keep their ideals to themselves. They have seen too many clashes between vision and bureaucracy or too many grand schemes that went nowhere, and have reached the cynical conclusion that educational bandwagons are usually drawn by a team of white elephants.

Yet Michael Rose, visiting classrooms across the country, found that most of the teachers he observed had a strong belief in the worth and potential of all their students and were willing to "push on the existing order of things" to help realize that potential. Perhaps, as Barth suggests, the vision has not died but is merely kept from view, a private possession rather than a public commitment.

The leadership challenge is to make conversation about ideals a regular, valued part of professional interaction. Principals can do this primarily by the power of their own example. If they set aside time at faculty meetings for such questions, it sends an important message; if in their daily interactions they give ideals equal standing with budgets, schedules, and reports, it empowers teachers to bring their own visions out of hiding.

3. *Encouraging Innovation.* Even before the written vision takes shape, the discussion may stimulate teachers to experiment with new approaches. The principal can send the signal, through innumerable small actions, that acting on personal vision is not only permitted but encouraged. Teachers get the message:

> The principal is very receptive to new ideas and ways of doing things. She values the opinions of all her staff members. She realizes that our school and our students are unique and welcomes suggestions and ideas for improving instruction. We have an instructional task force that continually teaches new methods of instruction and we are encouraged to try new techniques. (Blase and Blase 1994)

Blase and Blase emphasize that it is important for teachers to be able to carry out this experimentation in a nonthreatening environment, without fear of criticism when ideas don't work.

4. *Inspiring Others.* Kouzes and Posner note that most people don't consider themselves inspiring but that they can have inspirational effects by being emotionally expressive:

> Expressiveness comes naturally to people talking about deep desires for the future. They lean forward in their chairs, they move their arms about, their eyes light up, their voices sing with emotion, and a smile appears on their faces. In these circumstances, people are enthusiastic, articulate, optimistic, and uplifting.

In part, then, inspiration is a matter of expressive style; words and gestures that convey enthusiasm and excitement are likely to be contagious. Kouzes and Posner add, however, that this is not something that can be simulated; the leader's convictions must be genuine.

5. *Finding the Common Ground.* Personal dreams take tangible shape when we realize they are shared by others. As leaders talk with teachers, they should be listening for the common ground, looking for the signs that say, "This is what this school is about!" Kouzes and Posner say:

> Leaders find the common thread that weaves the fabric of human needs into a colorful tapestry. They develop a deep understanding of the collective yearnings; they seek out the brewing consensus among those they would lead. They listen carefully for quiet whisperings in dark corners and attend to subtle cues. They get a sense of what people want, what they value, what they dream about.

Those signs are out there, in words, stories, body language, and most of all in actions. Leaders can find them if they look, if they devote enough time to roaming the hallways and talking to teachers, students, and parents.

As leaders begin to sense the areas of consensus, they can feed their impressions back to the faculty, helping them confirm vague impressions and sparking further reflection and discussion.

6. *Keeping a Positive, Uplifting Focus.* The power of a vision is its ability to help people feel they are part of something special, part of an effort that is not just going to make improvements but transform their work. William Cunningham and Donn Gresso argue that developing a vision should not be looked on as merely a matter of solving problems:

> Problem-solving creates a group dynamic of defensiveness, protectionism, power struggle, mistrust, and an ultimately adversarial relationship. Applied to the improvement of schooling, the model usually results in feelings of failure, incompetence, and depression.... A sense of inadequacy develops within the culture.

A visionary approach, they say, puts aside the need to justify failures and instead asks, "Where do we go from here?"

Even simple language habits may make a difference. Kouzes and Posner urge leaders to say "will" rather than "try." They say this does not require being naive or unrealistic about the difficulties, which should be openly recognized. It is more a matter of projecting an attitude that says, "I'm confident we'll work through all the difficulties and reach the goal."

Starratt likewise points to the importance of language, noting that vision statements often employ vivid imagery that hits home. Metaphors that liken school to "gardening," "family," "symphonies,"and "journeys" will touch the heart as well as the mind.

7. *Dramatizing Core Beliefs.* As the vision begins to emerge, it will initially seem tentative and shaky; the leader's role is to dramatize it. As abstract statements of principles, visions may seem distant and unreachable; connected to the drama of human life, they take on deep meaning.

Terry Deal argues that organizational improvement takes on life when portrayed through metaphor, poetry, drama, stories, and rituals. For example, one of the things that lets teachers talk about visions at all is the occasional classroom encounter that makes a better future seem possible. Encouraging teachers to tell stories about these exciting moments is a good way to spread the excitement and make the vision seem reachable.

As noted earlier, something as simple as meeting offcampus can lend drama and significance to the effort. One experienced teacher, veteran of many a reform, observes that just once it would be nice to launch a change with a nice meal at a carpeted conference center instead of stale doughnuts in a drafty cafeteria.

SYNTHESIZING THE VISION

All these activities may lead a school closer to its vision, generating excitement and enthusiasm. Yet at some point the vision must be articulated and publicly disseminated.

Having created enthusiasm and a stimulating atmosphere in which teachers feel free to experiment, principals may be tempted to let things ride. After all, isn't our vision truly in what we do rather than what we say?

And surely there are risks in committing words to paper. Part of the early excitement in vision formation is the sense of unlimited possibilities, the implicit belief that we can do it all. Stating the vision forces a choice between equally attractive futures; teachers who believed the vision would incorporate their own philosophy may be dismayed to find their colleagues leaning in another direction. Moreover, stating the vision produces accountability. Having said it, we are now expected to do it.

Yet a vision that is not clearly articulated is a vision that is likely to wither. The initial excitement may carry people for a while but eventually the usual mundane concerns (which never seem to go away) begin to crowd out the experimentation; the inevitable missteps may discourage some, causing them to put their ideas on hold. Through all that, the existence of a written statement helps keep the vision real.

However, there is no need to produce the statement according to any particular schedule. Nanus suggests allowing time for ideas to simmer. The steering committee can slowly start to sketch out possibilities; at some point, they can draw up alternative visions, write them out, and share them with others.

How does one know the statement is ready? Here again there is no textbook answer, just a need for finely tuned professional judgment. Nanus suggests some possible criteria, saying the vision should be:

- future oriented

- utopian (leading to a better future)

- appropriate for the organization

- reflective of high ideals and excellence

- indicative of the organization's direction

- capable of inspiring enthusiasm

- reflective of the organization's uniqueness

- ambitious

Other commentators reinforce many of these points. For example, James Collins and Jerry Porras emphasize the importance of setting ambitious targets. They found that visionary companies have a habit of establishing "big hairy audacious goals." They cite numerous examples, such as Henry Ford's vision of a car so affordable that anyone could aspire to own one, or Walt Disney's dream of a feature-length animated cartoon based on a fairy tale—goals that seemed highly unlikely at the time they were adopted.

Hammer and Stanton adopt a slightly different angle on this issue by advocating "the Rule of Whacko," which means that "any valuable new process design will at first appear to be whacko." Ideas that immediately seem plausible are likely to represent small-scale tinkering at the edges; if, on the other hand, "you initially feel a new idea is ridiculous, absurd, and out of the question, our advice is: Look at it again, for it holds at least the potential of being important."

Virtually all experts on vision agree that the vision must in some way express the uniqueness of the organization, distinguishing *this* school from others. Many vision statements are rather vague, stating something like, "Generic Elementary School aims at meeting the needs of each child in a safe nurturing environment, and developing the skills to live in a democratic society." Compare that with the vision statement developed by Mt. Healthy Elementary School in Columbus, Indiana:

> *"Let all people become all that they were created capable of being; expand if possible to their full growth... and show themselves at length in their own shape and stature, be these what they may."* This is the educational vision of Mt. Healthy Elementary School. To attain this vision the Mt. Healthy staff creates a rich, challenging, supportive learning environment. A multi-sensory instructional approach is used that is designed to develop each child's full range of talents. Students are taught to think, generate information, analyze situations, work cooperatively and demonstrate ability to apply knowledge to problem solving situations. There is a major focus on experiential learning with the child as an active participant in his/her own education. The learning environment is expanded beyond the classroom through an outdoor lab, field experiences, mentors, and technology.

Simply put, a good vision allows us to *see*. Vivid language also keeps the vision's future thrust in clear view. Warm fuzzy statements are too easy to treat as descriptions (what we do) rather than goals (what we are striving to become). The statement does not exist just to make us feel good but to serve as a reminder of how far we have to go.

Good visions are also *moral* in purpose and in effect. It is easy to be seduced by futuristic images of fully wired schools where students have individual computers and freely roam the information superhighway, but the ultimate question that visions must answer is: "For what?" As Starratt notes, the whole point of having schools is to help form better people and better societies.

But the best sign of a ripe vision may be in the emotions it arouses. Bennis and colleagues quote Kevin Kingsland:

> When you have found your vision you do not ask yourself whether you have one. You inform the world about it. If you're wondering whether you have a vision, then you haven't got one. When you've discovered your vision you abound with inspiration. Your eyes sparkle. You can see it in the atmosphere. It is pulsing with life.

FIVE

LIVING THE VISION

Having formulated a written statement, there is, at least psychologically, a pause for breath. The statement is a considerable achievement that should be recognized and celebrated before moving on to the next step.

And there *is* a next step. One of the major errors in vision-building is confusing the statement with the vision. In their work with businesses, Michael Hammer and Steven Stanton have found that the official statement is usually given a major publicity blitz, in memos, posters, and wallet-sized laminated cards (not to mention key rings, buttons, and notebook covers). Unfortunately, they say, this effort is often wasted on empty slogans or feel-good words like "excellence," "integrity," or "teamwork." The problem is not that the visions are wrong, but that they never become more than attractive rhetoric encased in plastic.

Similarly, schools sometimes seem to view the statement as *evidence* of excellence rather than as a call for change. Educators see themselves as already working hard to fulfill the lofty goals in the vision, so the statement is offered as a kind of reassurance that things are on the right track. Discrepancies between the imperfect present and the ideal future are easy to overlook.

In reality, visions do little good unless they are used, not only in everyday conversations but in the dozens of daily decisions that make up the life of the school. In other words, they must be *institutionalized*. This chapter examines two major components of this process: (1) realigning structures to support the vision and (2) integrating the vision into the school's culture.

REALIGNING STRUCTURES TO SUPPORT
THE VISION

If teaching is the heart of a school, administrative structures and policies are the skeleton that supports it. Budgeting, scheduling, policy enforcement, and contract administration are unglamorous tasks that have a major impact on what happens in the classroom.

Starratt visualizes the school as an onion. At the core are the beliefs, assumptions, goals, and myths that are the source of vision. The outer layers are composed of policies (the basic rules governing organizational behavior), programs (the division of the school's work into departments, grade levels, and offices), organization (the distribution of resources through budgets, schedules, and staffing), and operations (the visible work of classroom teaching and learning).

Unless the outer layers are infused with the spirit and implications of the core values, and aligned with the goals, the vision is unlikely to last or have an impact on student learning. For example, if a middle school seeks to develop a team approach, it must adjust the schedule so teachers on the same team have common planning time. Likewise, a commitment to technological literacy will require acquisition of considerable hardware, and a shift to whole-language instruction will be undermined if the school continues to emphasize achievement tests closely linked to basal readers.

As Starratt describes it, integrating the vision and the organization seems to require ambidextrous principals. With one hand, they administer, managing materials and resources to get the job done; with the other, they lead, nurturing the organization's soul.

A SYSTEMS PERSPECTIVE

Implementation is the crunch step, the phase in which many visions begin to wither. This is true for all types of organizations, but schools are notorious for failing to follow through. The scenario is familiar: a change is inaugurated with trumpets and fanfare, creating great enthusiasm. Then problems begin popping up, answers are hard to find, a more urgent priority crowds out the old agenda, and a few years later old-timers reminisce, "Oh yeah, 1994—that was the year we did authentic assessment."

Why does this happen so often? Certainly, there are times when the change has been poorly thought out, or is simply tossed in the laps of teachers without any intention of administrative follow-through. But in most cases, the reason is more subtle: organizations are complex environments, consisting of multiple parts that interact unpredictably—and sometimes irrationally.

Peter Senge emphasizes that organizations are *systems*—a change in one part of the organization is likely to provoke reactions from other parts. He has described a number of common situations ("archetypes") that typify system relationships gone awry. For example, one archetype is "the tragedy of the commons," in which people work diligently but in isolation, accomplishing individual responsibilities well but failing to address issues that have mutual ownership. In schools this frequently happens with curriculum articulation; each teacher is responsible for helping students meet the goals that are established, but no one feels responsible for asking what the goals should be and how well students are prepared for the next level.

Another archetype that shows up frequently in reform efforts is "shifting the burden," in which a "hero" steps in to solve a problem that should be handled by someone else. The short-term result is positive, since the immediate problem goes away. However, the organization's long-term ability to solve problems is hurt because both the rescuer and the rescued grow comfortable with the arrangement, and problem-solving skills atrophy. When the rescuer moves on, the organization has to start over.

In schools, the most likely hero is the principal. Blase and Blase (1997) note that leaders trying to implement shared decision-making are often pressured (or tempted) to revert to a more hierarchical approach in moments of stress. One principal reflected that sharing power can create self-doubts:

> You have a tendency to want to go in with guns blazing to show that you've still got it; I've done that on an occasion or two. You get tired, and you start to feel like you're kind of left out, and then suddenly a minor issue comes along and you just hit it with both barrels. Well, it creates more problems than it's worth.

Senge notes that archetypes are deeply ingrained patterns of thought, making it hard for participants to see how they may be undercutting the very reforms they are working so hard to implement.

Leithwood and Aitken, endorsing the systems perspective, point out that many educational innovations focus only on "first-order" changes (curricular and instructional practices) while ignoring "second-order" changes (organizational structure, policies, and culture). For example, a district may wish teachers to use more active forms of learning in the classroom, but it continues to use a teacher-evaluation form that puts a premium on direct instruction. Or, a project may be launched with great fanfare but no provisions for staffing (teachers are expected to somehow fit the new tasks into their current schedule).

Systems tend to be self-preserving; new ideas that don't fit into the current equilibrium get squeezed out. Leithwood and Aitken note that some innovations are gradually worn down until they look like the rest of the system while others are "surrounded and repulsed in much the same way that white blood cells deal with foreign organisms in the bloodstream."

However, concentrating on second-order changes does not necessarily improve the situation. For example, numerous studies have shown that shared decision-making (a second-order change) does not automatically result in significant changes in instructional practices (Lynn Liontos and Larry Lashway). Rather, principals must consciously strive to link first-order and second-order changes. In particular, the vision will have implications for goal-setting, decision-making, training, budgeting, and monitoring.

GOAL-SETTING

Visions imply action: if the desired future is in *this* direction, we ought to be taking *these* steps. Thus, an immediate consequence of any vision should be a candid assessment of the current reality. For example, if the future direction includes a strong emphasis on critical thinking and problem-solving, these questions can be asked:

- What do we mean by critical thinking and problem-solving? How would we recognize it when we see it?

- How are our students currently doing in this area? What evidence do we have?

- What are we currently doing that provides a good foundation for critical thinking and problem-solving? What evidence do we have that this is a good foundation?

- What are we currently doing (or failing to do) that hinders the development of critical thinking and problem-solving?

- What steps could we take as a school in the coming year to move us closer to the vision? What steps could we take as individuals?

This process could be carried out by a steering committee, the site council, or an entirely new group.

DECISION-MAKING

A vision can be born in the mind of a single leader and sold to an entire organization through skillful communication. But at some point it will either become the property of the entire organization or it will die. No vision is so complete that it will survive in the classroom without being changed, redirected, or adapted to fit reality.

Thus it is difficult to imagine visions succeeding without some form of shared decision-making (SDM). The sharing may be formal or informal, though in most cases there will some kind of steering committee or site council to channel the decisions. The details of the arrangement are probably less important than the ability to learn new roles and question old assumptions about leadership (Liontos and Lashway).

However, attention to certain structural issues will facilitate the shift in behavior. First, the role of the steering committee or site council should be clearly outlined. Will they be the primary decision-makers, or will their role be to advise and recommend? If there is a special group overseeing the vision, how does it relate to the site council or to the faculty at large? Will decisions be made by consensus or formal voting?

Second, committee members should be well versed in collaborative problem-solving and team-building techniques. In most cases, they will require special training to fill the role effectively (Dolan).

Third, free-flowing communication between the core group and the rest of the school community is just as important for implementation as it was for developing the vision. There must be built-in ways for the steering group to receive regular, systematic feedback on what is happening in the classroom. Is the vision well-understood? Are teachers able to translate it into specific instructional techniques? Is part of it proving unrealistic? Committees can use surveys and well-focused faculty forums to get this feedback. For example, if the grapevine hints that parents are confused by the new portfolio-based grading system, the committee could survey them to get more systematic feedback, and then devote one or more faculty meetings to resolving any identified trouble spots.

All of this attention to the decision-making process is time-consuming, but essential. No matter how inspiring the rhetoric, visions make a difference only when accompanied by sustained effort and experimentation.

TEACHER LEARNING

Visions often call for significant changes in classroom teaching methods; in turn, changes in *practice* usually require changes in *thinking*. Richard Elmore and colleagues, after extensive analysis of restructuring schools, concluded:

> Good teaching is not simply a matter of individual taste or style; it is a matter of deep, complex and hard-won understandings of how to construct teaching that is consistent with one's views of how children ought to learn.

They found that even teachers who enthusiastically embraced new ideas found it "extraordinarily difficult" to engage in the kind of sustained critical reflection that leads to new understandings. The new behaviors were often just slightly spiffed-up versions of traditional methodology.

Thus, leaders must give careful thought to providing support for the right kind of teacher learning. Elmore and his associates concluded that the standard one-shot presentations and prepackaged lessons were ineffective. What teachers required were experiences that exposed them to concrete demonstrations of new methods and that put them in touch with skilled mentors who could help them work through the difficulties.

Peer coaching, visits to model schools, teaming, and use of networks are all approaches that facilitate the necessary kind of learning. However, the precise form of the activities is probably less important than an environment in which collaboration and reflection are pervasive.

BUDGETING

One of the most challenging structural requirements for vision is channeling adequate resources to the appropriate areas. Financial support is important for symbolic as well as substantive reasons: when leaders fail to "put their money where their mouth is," teachers will assume that the change effort should not be taken seriously.

Some of the support needs will be obvious, such as equipment and professional development, but the most underfinanced need may be *time* (Blase and colleagues). Most visions ask teachers to work collaboratively with colleagues to reexamine the way they teach. Collaboration and reflection are not activities that can be parceled out in the fragmented moments that count as "free time" for teachers. Susan Moore Johnson (1990a) warns, "If local districts expect that they can reform school organization with their current funding and time allocations, they probably will fail."

At a time when school resources are already stretched thin, coming up with the money is a daunting task for any principal. Three avenues seem to be available:

1. *Reallocating existing budgetary funds to support the vision.* This is sometimes possible with professional-development money; rather than financing a scattershot program, the money can be focused to support the vision.

2. *Wringing extra dollars from the district.* Sometimes the central office controls funds that politically adept principals may be able to pry loose. This is particularly true if the school's vision seems to support district priorities.

3. *Relying on outside sources, such as business partnerships or state grants.* Many potential funders are attracted to a process that promises significant change.

However, Richard Ackerman and colleagues emphasize that in the end the money is always finite, and principals must be prepared for some tough decisions. They suggest that if the school has developed some form of collaborative decision-making, the budgeting dilemmas can be shared with a wider group. In that way, teachers will come to better understand the realities and be less likely to regard the lack of funding as a betrayal of the vision.

MONITORING

A well-crafted vision will take a school to places it has never been before—some of them quite unintended. Members of the school community will not only learn new things about their school, they will have to unlearn some things.

To make sense of the turbulence, schools must develop a monitoring system that will give them an objective snapshot of how the vision is affecting (or failing to affect) the organization.

Leithwood and Aitken recommend that schools use a wide array of indicators in tracking progress and making future decisions. Their list includes data on:

- inputs (the "givens" in a school environment, such as student and community characteristics)

- district and school characteristics (such as mission and goals, culture, core tasks, community partnerships, and so forth)

- outcomes (such as achievement, participation and engagement, equity, and equality)

Their book contains many sample assessment tools that could be easily adapted to the needs of individual schools.

Leithwood and Aitken emphasize the importance of actually using the data in the decision-making process. At some point, the steering committee (or whatever group is spearheading the vision) should examine the data systematically and determine what steps are necessary to keep the vision alive and growing.

REALIGNING THE SCHOOL'S CULTURE

Most school reformers have learned (often through hard experience) that successful change is not just a matter of shuffling Xs and Os on the organization chart. Schools are living communities that behave in unique and sometimes surprising ways.

In recent years, researchers have pointed to the school's *culture* as a key to change efforts. Conley defines the term this way:

Basically, the culture of a school is the way people think about things, the way they do things, and the way they interact based on those beliefs and activities—all the rules and roles, formal and informal. It is how people treat one another, how they think about their role in the larger group, how they handle conflict and celebration, and how they communicate—the rituals and myths, the collective history, and the storytelling and gossiping.

Although the effect of culture is hard to measure directly, most school reformers consider it to be a powerful influence.

The relationship between vision and culture has not been thoroughly explored, but it is undoubtedly complex. On the one hand, a vision that has been collectively generated by teachers, and enthusiastically accepted, should already be aligned with the school's culture. On the other hand, teachers may not have thought out all the implications of the vision or they may have an oversimplified idea of what it will take to get there. There is always the chance that movement toward the vision will clash with long-established ways of thinking and behaving.

For example, many vision statements take a rather expansive view of human potential: "We believe that all students can learn," they say, or, "Our goal is to help each individual reach his or her maximum potential." Yet teachers who endorse that statement without batting an eye will also tell you (discreetly), "There are some students who just can't learn." Unable to break through to certain students, they assume that the problem is beyond the school's power.

Another powerful cultural barrier is the professional norm that says, "Teachers don't tell colleagues how to teach." This "live and let live" mentality, which has deep historical roots, makes frank discussions of methods difficult, especially when the implication is that some methods are preferable to others (Griffin).

A FRAMEWORK FOR VIEWING CULTURE

Culture is a broad concept that seems to reach into every area of school life, so analysis can be difficult. One useful tool comes from Lee Bolman and Terry Deal (1991), who argue that organizations can be viewed through four "frames." Frames are simply perspectives: cognitive filters that highlight certain features of the organization.

The *structural* frame emphasizes the rules, policies, and procedures that provide the skeleton holding a school together. Through this structure, the school formulates goals, makes plans to achieve them, and evaluates progress. The ultimate goal is coordination and control through rational analysis.

The *human-resource* frame recognizes the human needs of employees, paying close attention to relationships, feelings, and motivation; the goal is to make the workplace congenial and rewarding.

The *political* frame sees the school as an arena in which people continually jockey for power and resources to protect what is important to them. The result is a nonstop process of coalition-building, lobbying, bargaining, and compromise (much of it behind the scenes).

The *symbolic* frame focuses on the meaning of events as expressed through myths, heroes, stories, and sacred rituals. It recognizes that organizations play a role in the lives of employees that cannot be captured through organization charts and policy manuals.

The remainder of this chapter is organized around the insights that each frame offers for understanding the relationship between culture and vision.

Vision Through a Structural Frame

The first section of this chapter has already described how vision can be supported by realigning organizational structures such as decision-making, budgeting, and monitoring. However, these structures not only have a material impact on the vision, they can influence the culture's attitude toward it.

For example, a principal who replaces routine announcements with reflective discussion at faculty meetings is not only providing precious time for collaborative discussion, he or she is sending a powerful message about organizational priorities. Likewise, a principal who reallocates scarce money to support a teacher visit to another school is elevating the status of the vision in everyone's eyes. When structures are aligned to support the vision, the culture is forced to take it seriously.

Vision Through a Human-Resources Frame

Vision calls on people to change, and the human response to change is never simple. Even if the vision has been developed openly and collaboratively, there will always be those who lack enthusiasm and commitment. Dolan estimates that for most major changes, 10 percent of the teachers will be flatly opposed, 20-25 percent will be in favor, and the rest will be skeptical but willing to be convinced.

Sources of Resistance

Mihaly Csikszentmihalyi notes that the conservative, self-preserving side of human nature is more deeply rooted than the adventuresome, innovative side. People require a certain amount of stability to meet the challenges of each day; too much change, too fast, evokes strong reactions. Management consultant William Bridges (1991) points out that sudden change plunges people into a major psychological transition. He outlines three stages:

- First, every new beginning is actually an *ending* that requires letting go of the old order, sometimes even inducing a grieving process.

- Second is a *neutral zone* that represents a kind of limbo in which the old way is gone and the new isn't yet comfortable.

- Finally comes the actual new *beginning*, in which the new way begins to seem natural and normal.

Bridges argues that all three stages are necessary and ultimately healthful; they need to be properly managed, not avoided.

Some resistance has more specific causes. Paul Strebel argues that change is always suspect because it threatens the implicit "compact" that exists between employees and the organization. Workers are uncomfortable when they are unable to answer certain basic questions about expectations:

- What am I supposed to do for the organization?

- What help will I get to do the job?

- How and when will I be evaluated?

- What will I be paid?

- How hard will I really have to work?

- What recognition or satisfaction will I get?

- Are the rewards worth the effort?

- Are my values shared by others in the organization?

- What are the real rules for success in this organization?

Many of these questions are never answered explicitly by the organization, but over time employees work out the answer. When a major change looms on the horizon, the compact is put at risk. In many cases, change agents haven't thought about the organizational implications of the change or simply don't know what the effects will be. Because these questions are seldom discussed openly, employees are left to stew over things on their own. At times, the anxiety surfaces as skepticism, sullen compliance, or open resistance.

At other times, resistance is a matter of honest philosophical disagreement. There are those on every faculty who gravitate toward child-centered, open-ended environments, while others believe in highly structured, academically oriented approaches. Ironically, those who care the most about what they do may be the strongest opponents of the new vision.

Some resistance is simply good sense. As Andrew Gitlin and Frank Margonis point out, when a proposed change imposes extra burdens on teachers without providing additional resources, resistance is just a way of saying "This is unrealistic."

Finally, some resistance is rooted in the nature of teaching, which is a complex activity filled with uncertainty (Joseph Shedd and Samuel Bacharach); in any given case, a teacher can never be completely sure of the right thing to do. Moreover, teachers do not control major decisions such as scheduling, textbooks, and grading policies, so the control they do have—things such as pacing and choice of specific methods—is guarded jealously (Larry Cuban).

Faced with these constraints, teachers filter new ideas through a stringent standard—what some have called "the practicality ethic" (Fullan with Stiegelbauer):

- Does the change fill a need? How will it be accepted by students? Is there evidence it works?

- Does the change clearly spell out what the teacher must do?

- How will it personally affect the teacher in terms of time, effort, excitement, and interference with existing priorities?

- How rewarding will it be in terms of interaction with peers?

Unless teachers can be convinced that the answers to these questions will be positive, they are unlikely to integrate the idea into their repertoire.

Whatever the cause of resistance, Hammer and Stanton caution leaders against looking for logical reasons. "Ultimately, it is how people feel about a new situation that determines how they will respond to it. If they feel frightened, or threatened, or uncomfortable, or uncertain, then their reaction is likely to be a negative one."

Responding to Resistance

Hammer and Stanton point out that resistance is actually a positive sign, an indicator that something significant is happening. It is a natural human response, not a sign that the vision is somehow deficient.

Yet resistance presents leaders with a sensitive human-relations dilemma. On the one hand, the vision embodies the core values of the school and demands allegiance from everyone who chooses to work there. While the vision should allow teachers reasonable autonomy and flexibility, it also makes certain nonnegotiable demands. Sergiovanni says, "It is the leader's responsibility to be outraged when empowerment is abused and when purposes are ignored."

When teachers conspicuously fail to honor those purposes, or continually disparage and demean the vision, or even settle for passive resistance, they spread a contagious dampening cloud over the whole project.

On the other hand, directly confronting the resisters doesn't always work. For one thing, direct confrontations can escalate into dramatic showdowns that tenured teachers seldom lose. Moreover, such drastic action may, in the long run, be counterproductive; even teachers who support the vision may be unnerved by the idea that there is a "politically correct" view that affects job security.

The other problem is that the deepest resistance is beneath the surface, often cleverly disguised as sweet reason and cooperation. Hammer and Stanton list some common forms:

- Denial. ("What problem?" This is especially common in organizations that are not yet in crisis, when it is still possible to explain away the signs of decline.)

- Debunking. ("We tried that years ago, and it didn't work.")

- Stalling. ("Great idea, but we've got three other initiatives going right now and we really can't give it the time it deserves. Let's take a look at it next year.")

- "The Kiss of Yes." (People agree but never follow through.)

Hammer and Stanton put it this way: "Never try to teach a pig how to sing; it wastes your time, and annoys the pig. Along the same lines, never try arguing logic with someone in a state of total inner panic." Instead, they recommend dealing with the underlying anxieties, not the symptoms.

A similar note is sounded by Bridges (1991), who does not attribute resistance to animosity or stubbornness, but to normal human psychology (even among those who support the change). He suggests a number of approaches that may be helpful to people in the midst of a transition.

1. *Identify what the resisters may have lost.* It may be a position of influence or status; it may be a philosophical allegiance (for example, a teacher who has long prided herself on teaching the basics may feel abandoned as the school moves toward a whole-language approach).

2. *Honor what is being lost.* The old ways may no longer be appropriate for the new century, but in their day they may have served many children well. The need for new directions does not mean that those using the old ways have wasted their lives.

3. *Mark the endings.* People often cope with change through ceremonies (funerals, birthdays, graduations) that dramatically and publicly announce the new order.

4. *Emphasize the continuity in the new vision.* As noted earlier, a good vision will build on the organization's past. The vision may be a shift in course, but it's still the same ship.

5. *Publicly recognize the inner turmoil that everyone is experiencing.* People are often reluctant to talk about confusion and negative feelings, thereby denying themselves the comfort and counsel of others. Leaders must set the tone by being open and honest about their own confusions and uncertainties (though never to the point of doubting the vision), as well as being sensitive to the uncertainties of others.

6. *Make sure that everyone has a part to play.* This means that they not only understand what changes the vision requires of them but

have an opportunity to take part in the vision process. As people invest time and effort in a goal, they begin to acquire a psychological stake in its success.

7. *Be consistent.* The vision calls for certain new behaviors and attitudes, which should be implemented and rewarded. Principals can be sure that teachers will be watching closely; failing to act with the vision may be taken as a sign of wavering or even hypocrisy.

8. *Strive for early successes, even small ones.* In the early stages of implementation, when not everyone is fully convinced, results are often magnified out of proportion to their actual importance. By highlighting certain low-risk tasks, or arranging for some long-sought concession or resource from higher authorities, leaders can score important points when it most matters. Bridges (1991) says, "Quick successes reassure the believers, convince the doubters, and confound the critics."

A final thought on resistance is added by Michael Fullan and Matthew Miles, who point out that people adapt to change at different rates. The leader, who has probably been working with the new vision longer than anyone, may have already made the psychological transition, working out new patterns of meaning over a long period. To expect others to reach the same point overnight is to treat them as puppets.

Vision Through a Political Frame

No matter how people feel about a vision, they generally watch it closely because their interests are at stake:

> Members of an organization want to protect and enhance their careers. Local merchants are concerned with the prosperity of the neighborhood. Bureaucrats, administrators, teachers, and parents have desires for power, prestige, concrete advantage, comfort, safety and other good things. (Carol Weiss)

The self-interest can be ideological as well as material. People are committed to certain beliefs, values, and practices, and they will maneuver to have the school follow those standards (or at least not interfere with them).

These interests are played out in the school's political arena, where the principal is deeply involved as a participant and as a facilitator.

The Principal as Politician

Like everyone else in the school, principals have interests to protect, many of which are affected by the vision. Rightly or wrongly, they are held accountable for whatever happens in their schools; a high-profile vision that goes awry will threaten their professional reputations (and sometimes their job security).

Fullan and Stiegelbauer have pointed out that principals are under great pressure to maintain stability in the school. Under the best of circumstances, a principal's day is filled with efforts to smooth over conflicts, put out brush fires, and generally keep things on an even keel. No matter how exciting the prospects for transforming the school, a vision threatens whatever hard-won equilibrium the principal has established. Thus, school leaders find themselves torn between pushing the organization to change and pulling in the reins when the change goes too far, too fast. In the words of one principal:

> It's a lot of give and take—knowing when to assert yourself and when to sit back and allow others to take charge. You balance things, and each situation is different. (Blase and Blase 1997)

Principals push in a variety of ways.

1. *Appealing to teacher professionalism.* William Greenfield argues that in schools "moral sources of influence are more inviting and more enduring than influence based upon other types of power." This is particularly true if teachers (who are an idealistic lot) can be led to see the connection between the vision and the goals that brought them into teaching in the first place.

2. *Relentless reflective questioning.* The visionary principal described by Marlene Johnson hooked teachers by continually asking open-ended questions: What would happen if we did this? What's our purpose here? Where are we trying to go? Apparently, the barrage of questions, combined with the principal's willingness to admit she didn't have the answers, spurred teachers to seek answers for themselves.

3. *Cultivating opinion leaders.* Every faculty has a few people who, because of longevity or perceived expertise, have considerable

influence over their peers. Sounding them out about key issues can not only elicit good advice, it may also pull them into the process—if not as active supporters, at least as benign observers.

4. *Holding the line.* As flexible as the vision may be, there is always some point at which the line must be drawn. There are many ways to get to the same goal, but not every way is appropriate. Sometimes principals must step in (or let teachers *think* they will intervene) when the vision's core values are threatened. Ultimately, they may have to go as far as pressuring certain teachers into looking for more congenial surroundings.

The Principal as Facilitator

Beyond their own interests in the vision, principals are managers of the school's political arena. In this role, they have to step back from advocacy and become facilitators. The vision often unleashes great energies, as teachers feel empowered to pursue exciting new ideas. These efforts may produce conflicting interpretations of the vision or lead teachers to compete for scarce resources, generating disputes that must be resolved.

Acting as a facilitator, the principal:

- works with teachers and parents to mediate conflicts

- acts as liaison with the community to explain and defend the vision

- lobbies district officials to supply necessary resources and to protect the integrity of the vision

In addition, principals facilitate the vision by modeling certain qualities in one-to-one interactions. Marshall Sashkin has found five specific kinds of behavior to be important: communicating effectively (for example, using active listening); expressing the vision in exciting and attention-getting ways; maintaining consistency of purpose and actions (no waffling or vacillation); showing respect for oneself and others; and creating "sensible risks" (aiming for high but attainable goals).

VISION THROUGH A SYMBOLIC FRAME

For most people, work is not just a way of making money, but a major part of who they are and how they make sense of their lives.

The symbolic frame zeroes in on the *meaning* of organizational life and the kind of symbols that people use to affirm that meaning.

Vision, when it has been publicly stated and accepted, is a potent symbol of what the school stands for. As such, it becomes a source of strength and inspiration. However, the vision itself can be nurtured by thoughtful use of symbolism.

1. *Tell the vision as a story.* Story-telling is a uniquely human trait found in every culture and is a primary way that people make sense out of their lives. Howard Gardner says that one of the key functions of leadership is telling a story about the organization that helps followers find meaning in what they do. Because the vision points to the destination of a journey, it is already an implicit story: we are the characters, the vision provides our motive, and the plot is what happens to us as we move toward the goal. Told that way, the vision becomes a compelling tale of human struggle, not just an abstract academic goal. A compressed version of the story might look something like this:

> As a school, we've always prided ourselves on high academic standards and student achievement, but in recent years we've begun to wonder whether we're preparing our students for the challenges they'll face. After long discussion, we've decided to move in the direction of *x*. We want to produce graduates who have these qualities, and here's the way we'll do it.

As the vision unfolds, of course, the plot will thicken, with many unexpected twists and turns along the way. Such a story, fleshed out with the human-interest details that all good stories contain, can be highly effective in gaining support for the vision.

2. *Tell stories about the vision.* An effective vision will launch all kinds of little classroom experiments, some of which will be wildly successful, others of which will encounter setbacks. Encouraging teachers to share those stories publicly will not only help people process what is happening but will create a shared bond. (The success stories are inspirational, of course, but even the "setback" stories can be validating as a tangible reminder of the common struggle. Stories that tell of student responses to the new methods often add zest and humor to the effort.)

3. *Recognize the heroes.* Every change effort has heroes and heroines who blaze the trail and take the biggest risks. Those efforts deserve recognition, both as a psychic reward for the pioneers and as

inspiration for others. In school settings, administrative recognition requires a deft touch; because of teaching's egalitarian culture, singling out teachers for public praise can create resentment (Ann Bradley). The most important kind of reward may be knowledge that the principal knows and appreciates what the teacher is doing. One teacher put it this way:

> The principal is aware of the hours I keep and of the constant communication I attempt with my learners and their families. This helps me feel like her colleague, her peer. I'm not just some hired help that comes and goes. (Blase and Blase 1994)

4. *Integrate ceremonies and rituals into the change effort.* People respond to visible "markers" that affirm the value and meaning of their work. Terry Deal tells of a principal leading an outdoor staff retreat who asked each teacher to write on a piece of wood a personal behavior or attitude they would give up to make the school a better place. Teachers read what they had written, and then tossed the wood into a large bonfire, symbolically consuming the negativity. (However, even informal rituals, such as the pizza order that caps the weekly steering committee meeting, can strengthen the process.)

5. *Don't stop talking about the vision.* Kotter says that most visions are drastically undercommunicated. In any organization, employees are awash in a sea of words, and what they hear about the vision is likely to comprise only a very small percentage. Confining vision-talk to a few meetings, speeches, or memos will have little impact. Only when the vision becomes part of the daily discussion will it have a chance to make inroads into the culture.

Kotter emphasizes that the communication need not be lengthy— a minute here, five minutes there: it adds up quickly and has a repetitive impact. He also emphasizes the importance of avoiding jargon, using multiple forums, and keeping the conversation flowing in both directions.

6. *Lead by example.* This is one of the oldest leadership maxims on the books, and one of the most important. When leaders *live* the vision, in action as well as words, it carries enormous symbolic weight.

FINAL THOUGHTS

As important as it is to transform the culture, Kotter urges leaders not to be overambitious:

Culture is not something that you manipulate easily. Attempts to grab it and twist it into a new shape never work, because you can't grab it. Culture changes only after you have successfully altered people's actions, after the new behavior produces some group benefit for a period of time, and after people see the connection between the new actions and the performance improvement.

In other words, cultural change occurs near the end, not the beginning, of the vision process. Indeed, a school that has changed its culture has probably come close to achieving the vision.

SIX

BEYOND VISION: THE LEARNING ORGANIZATION

Time to take stock. The vision is well on the road to success. Teachers are excited, parents are supportive, and students are beginning to respond. Now what? Is the school approaching a new—and better—status quo, or do more surprises lie ahead?

Whatever the hope, chances are that the *new* paradigm won't last nearly as long as the last one did. All indicators point to a continuing period of social, economic, and cultural change that will fully challenge the leadership skills of principals. Peter Vaill calls it "permanent white water": complex, messy, and full of surprises. The day may come when today's futuristic, exciting vision looks anemic and out of touch. What can you do now to prepare for that time?

AN ACCELERATING SOCIETY

School reform is often visualized as a one-time event in which the current unsatisfactory status quo is broken up, reshaped in the desired direction, and "refrozen" as a new status quo. This view assumes that the school has failed to keep up with changing times but that the environment will somehow stabilize as soon as the reform takes place. However, many observers now argue that in an age of extremely rapid change, organizations must *continually* reshape themselves to fit new circumstances (Drucker 1994).

Thus, management experts advise leaders to "surf the wave," "embrace ambiguity," and "let your actions be governed by chaos theory." Some of this advice may reflect faddism, but the business literature is filled with concrete examples of companies that have been forced into radical change that an earlier generation would have thought impossible. A representative of 3M company says, "We used to take four days from getting raw material to putting the product on the truck, and now we take 25 minutes. It's still not good enough" (Randall White and colleagues).

Although sheltered (for now) from the turmoil of the market-place, schools have also felt the effects of widespread social change: a curriculum stretched to the breaking point; students who seem less motivated and less focused than ever; an aging population that is increasingly reluctant to finance schools at traditional levels. And whatever schools do in response, the public seems to keep saying, "It's still not good enough."

ORGANIZATIONS THAT LEARN

In an age of accelerating change, adaptability is a prime virtue. Organizations that can figure out where things are headed and adjust their own course accordingly are the ones that will survive and even thrive. Some analysts have suggested that certain organizations be-come unusually adept at this. Collins and Porras, for example, have identified these characteristics of highly successful companies:

- They have strong organizational ideologies ("cult-like cultures").

- They have towering ambitions ("big hairy audacious goals").

- They ceaselessly experiment ("try a lot of stuff and keep what works").

- They develop their own leaders ("home grown management").

- They keep trying to top themselves ("good enough never is").

In short, these companies are *learning organizations* that see change not as a threat but as an incentive to become even better.

In the last decade, the notion of organizations that learn has intrigued a growing number of management experts. They suggest it is not enough to have employees become increasingly skilled at an individual level. Their learning should increase the *organization's* capacity to respond to change and advance its collective goals. Leithwood and Aitken define *learning organization* this way:

a group of people pursuing common purposes (individual purposes as well) with a collective commitment to regularly weighing the value of those purposes, modifying them when that makes sense, and continuously developing more effective and efficient ways of accomplishing those purposes.

In other words, significant learning is tied to common purpose. An employee who has learned a better way of doing things will not fully benefit the organization unless there are ways the new knowledge can be shared with others and become part of the collective repertoire.

What does a learning organization look like? Boyd and Hord offer this description of a school they studied:

> This is a place where children are valued, respected, cared for. Voices from the faculty portray this difference. "We are here for the children, not the other way around." Just as the children feel cared for, the faculty is nurtured. "We welcome people and take them to our hearts. There is a lot of spontaneity and creative work going on. Teachers help out parents and parents help out teachers—it's like a family."

Other schools may present this kind of happy face to the world, but when Boyd and Hord looked behind the scenes, they also found this:

> The entire faculty interacted with each other at a regularly scheduled time and place, spoke as one voice about their school and their role in it, shared a clear vision of what they wanted their school to be for children, participated in decision making, and practiced norms of critical inquiry regarding the effectiveness of their work and relationships with children.

Moreover, this school had apparently been operating in this manner for almost two decades; what the researchers found was not part of a one-shot reform effort.

Despite this attractive picture, there are reasons to be cautious about embracing the learning organization as the next great reform. The concept is not yet anchored to a firm theoretical foundation, and most of the evidence is anecdotal (Sandra Kerka). As far as schools are concerned, say Leithwood and colleagues, "we have almost no systematic evidence describing the conditions which foster and inhibit such learning." Nor, they add, is there any empirical evidence of improved student outcomes tied to organizational learning. The remainder of this chapter is based on the assumption that the learning organization offers an avenue worth exploring. However, any advice should be treated as informed speculation rather than conclusive recommendations.

(Principals who wish to reflect on their own school's status as a learning organization may find Survey 3 to be helpful.)

Survey 3

The following survey can be used to assess informally the degree to which teachers perceive the school as a learning organization. However, it should be regarded as a tool for provoking reflection rather than a valid scientific instrument.

Indicate the degree to which you believe the following statements to be true (1=strongly disagree, 5=strongly agree).

1. In the lounge, teachers frequently talk about curriculum and methods.

1————————2————————3————————4————————5

2. Teachers frequently observe in other classrooms.

1————————2————————3————————4————————5

3. Teachers have regular contact with peers in other schools in the district.

1————————2————————3————————4————————5

4. Teachers have regular contact with peers from outside the district.

1————————2————————3————————4————————5

5. Teachers who want to learn new approaches are given concrete support in the form of release time or funding for travel and conferences.

1————————2————————3————————4————————5

6. Teachers often operate in teams.

1————————2————————3————————4————————5

7. Teachers in this school are always trying new ideas in their classrooms.

1————————2————————3————————4————————5

8. When teachers are trying to solve a problem, they seek out help from peers or from district personnel.

1————————2————————3————————4————————5

9. Teachers have considerable leeway to make instructional decisions.

1————————2————————3————————4————————5

10. When teachers in this school want to try a new method, they don't feel they have to get permission from the office.

1————————2————————3————————4————————5

11. Successful innovations are recognized and celebrated by others in the school.

1————————2————————3————————4————————5

12. Teachers in this school have numerous professional development opportunities.

1————————2————————3————————4————————5

13. Within the past year, teachers from this school have visited classrooms in another school.

1————————2————————3————————4————————5

14. Teachers in this school pretty much agree on what good teaching is.

1————————2————————3————————4————————5

15. At faculty meetings, teachers often talk about what they're doing in their classrooms.

1————————2————————3————————4————————5

16. Within the past year, one or more teachers in this school have demonstrated a new teaching method to colleagues.

1————————2————————3————————4————————5

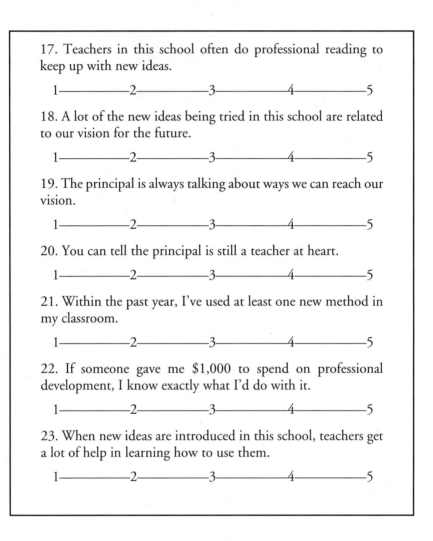

17. Teachers in this school often do professional reading to keep up with new ideas.

1————————2————————3————————4————————5

18. A lot of the new ideas being tried in this school are related to our vision for the future.

1————————2————————3————————4————————5

19. The principal is always talking about ways we can reach our vision.

1————————2————————3————————4————————5

20. You can tell the principal is still a teacher at heart.

1————————2————————3————————4————————5

21. Within the past year, I've used at least one new method in my classroom.

1————————2————————3————————4————————5

22. If someone gave me $1,000 to spend on professional development, I know exactly what I'd do with it.

1————————2————————3————————4————————5

23. When new ideas are introduced in this school, teachers get a lot of help in learning how to use them.

1————————2————————3————————4————————5

SCHOOLS AS LEARNING ORGANIZATIONS

One might expect that schools, as centers of learning, would be learning organizations, but there is plenty of evidence to the contrary. Nancy Isaacson and Jerry Bamburg conclude, "it is a stinging experience to read about LOs and realize how few schools and districts fit the definition." Peter Senge, asked if schools are learning organizations, says, "definitely not" (John O'Neil).

The reasons are complex, resulting from both the norms of the teaching profession and the working conditions in schools.

TEACHERS AS LEARNERS

Teachers are plunged every day into a fast-paced kaleidoscopic environment in which they can't rely on simple prescriptions to solve problems. Hendrik Gideonse notes that teachers are continually faced with difficult questions. What should I teach? How should I teach? What do these children know now? How shall I assess my students' learning? Is failure to learn the students' responsibility or mine? What's going on in this situation and how can I solve this problem?

In answering these questions, teachers cannot turn to an authoritative, publicly recognized body of knowledge. For a number of reasons, what teachers know is based more on personal experience than on shared expertise, and whatever one teacher has learned does not spread quickly to other teachers.

1. *Knowledge about teaching is tacit.* That is, the "right" decision depends on the context, is learned through experience, and cannot easily be reduced to explicit maxims. While experienced teachers have obviously learned a great deal about constructing lessons, motivating reluctant learners, managing unruly students, and explaining ideas clearly, their knowledge is highly individualized and difficult to share.

Consider the problem faced by Linda, a student teacher. One of her fourth-grade students was continually causing disturbances and was not responding to the usual admonitions. Discussion with the student revealed one point of leverage: he didn't want her to call his parents. So she made a deal: whenever he caused a disturbance, she would send a "secret signal" (tugging her ear) and as long as he settled down she wouldn't call his parents. It worked.

All in all, an elegant solution: the misbehavior diminished, the teacher was able to provide some positive attention, and the student took a step toward monitoring his own behavior. But what Linda learned about this student could not immediately be translated into a straightforward general rule. It might go into her "bag of tricks" as a possible solution to some future problem, but it certainly wouldn't work for all students. Similarly, the incident may be shared with other teachers as an interesting anecdote, but no one would expect ear-tugging to spread throughout the school as a disciplinary technique.

2. *Teachers have a strong sense of privacy about their work.* Because teaching is so dependent on context, teachers are usually reluctant to prescribe solutions for others or even raise questions about a colleague's practices. The result is that even when teachers collaborate, core classroom practices remain off-limits as an agenda item (Griffin).

3. *Teacher learning is dominated by a "practicality ethic."* If a new idea does not have obvious relevance to what teachers are currently doing, lacks clearcut procedural guidelines, or appears to require too much effort for too little gain, it will probably be ignored (Fullan and Stiegelbauer). Research-based knowledge is slow to spread, partly because it is disseminated through academic journals that teachers don't read and partly because teachers tend to be skeptical of abstract ideas that still have to be translated into classroom terms (Weiss).

SCHOOLS AS ENVIRONMENTS FOR LEARNING

While schools devote great energy to providing learning opportunities for students, they have often treated teacher learning as an afterthought. Conditions in many schools seem to discourage rather than support professional development.

1. *Schools cannot usually change course quickly.* Senge notes that unlike businesses, which have to answer only to the bottom line, schools are accountable to multiple constituencies—state agencies, parents, school boards—who are concerned not only with results but with the way results are achieved. Schools simply have less freedom to reinvent themselves.

For teachers, this means there is limited incentive—and some risk—for innovation. Even though they have a fair amount of latitude in making classroom decisions, no one can predict when a lesson or method will collide with public opinion or institutional policy. One teacher notes:

> The few teachers who are trying to be creative catch flak all the time from parents saying, "Wait a minute, we're trying to get Johnny to Harvard, and he has to reach these objectives, and you're trying to bring in something like thinking skills?" (Farkas and Johnson)

2. *Schools do not provide teachers with time to engage in extended reflection and inquiry.* Typically, teachers have less than an hour of unassigned time during the day, and that is usually taken up by

errands and phone calls. As one superintendent observes, "Teaching may be the only profession in which you have no time during the day to think about what you're doing."

3. *Teachers are physically isolated from one another.* Critics have often commented on the "cellular" or "eggcrate" structure that puts teachers in separate rooms with little chance for collegial interaction. Shedd and Bacharach found that of sixteen key teaching activities, only two involved contact with other adults, and those were typically either routine or hurried.

4. *Schools have often failed to provide resources for teacher learning.* Whereas many businesses routinely budget significant amounts for training, research, and development, schools rarely do. Funds for teacher training are given grudgingly, and are sometimes viewed suspiciously by the public (especially when they involve off-site learning opportunities). When budgets tighten, teacher training is often the first item to be slashed.

5. *Teacher training is sporadic, unfocused, and short-term.* Teachers often speak of the "reform du jour" that generates lots of discussion and a brief burst of training, only to fade from sight in a year or two. Many routinely expect that reform initiatives will soon disappear (Farkas and Johnson). Some potentially powerful changes— inclusive education, authentic assessment, whole language—may take years to be assimilated and understood, but teachers are typically given one-shot training with little followup during the all-important implementation phase.

Thus, the traditional school environment seems to suggest anything but a learning organization. Promising ideas come along often enough but are slow to be adopted; even when successfully adopted in one classroom, they don't spread easily to others. Teachers and administrators often have a weary sense of reinventing the wheel, as they recognize each "new" idea as a repackaged version of something that was tried years earlier. The difficulty so many schools have in reforming themselves is in part a failure of learning.

CREATING A LEARNING ORGANIZATION

If today's schools fall short of being learning organizations, what would it take to move them there? Research on learning organizations is too limited to provide a detailed roadmap, but the answer clearly involves more than increasing the professional development budget. Rather, schools must link learning to organizational purpose; pay close attention to the way people learn; establish a culture that nourishes learning; and maintain a clear focus in evaluating results.

VISION AS THE FOUNDATION

Learning organizations are not just schools in which teachers learn a lot by energetically pursuing their own agendas. Rather, they are engaged in a collective enterprise that adds up to more than the sum of its parts.

The fuel for this kind of synergy is shared vision, which becomes the reference point for raising questions and making decisions. If the vision points toward developing critical-thinking skills, then much of teachers' learning will be designed to explore the meaning of critical thinking and the ways it can be developed in students.

The cohesive effect of the vision not only influences the kinds of learning that teachers seek out, but it permeates daily conversation and interactions. Vision leads people to focus their mutual attention on issues that would otherwise be ignored, to share with others their efforts to put the vision into effect, and to challenge existing practices that are inconsistent with the vision. Elmore and colleagues describe one such school this way:

> Teachers agree on a fundamental level what good teaching practice is, while accepting important variations in the way it is actualized. They do not subscribe to the view that each teacher can have a distinctive "style" if it diverges from established good teaching practices, nor that teachers can disagree fundamentally on what good teaching is. It is precisely their common belief in certain basic principles that allows them to observe and capitalize on their differences.

Early studies of schools as learning organizations emphasize the importance of this kind of cohesion. However, Leithwood and colleagues (1995) caution that the sources of a shared sense of direction are not obvious or unambiguous. They found a few cohesive schools in which there was not a clear link between teacher learning and the principal's explicit vision-building activities. In those cases, the vision may have been implicitly modeled by the principal or embodied in the school's overall culture.

Future research may show more clearly how vision interacts with organizational learning. For now, school leaders should regard vision as a potentially powerful influence on learning, particularly if teachers currently show little consensus on purpose. However, the mere existence of a vision statement is not enough. According to Leithwood and colleagues (1995), it must be "clear, accessible, and widely shared by staff," must be perceived as meaningful, and must be pervasive in decision-making. Under those conditions, vision becomes a key factor in organizational learning.

NEW VIEWS OF LEARNING

The learning organization is a useful metaphor, but it is ultimately *people* who must learn and change their behavior. Providing training without paying attention to the needs and capacities of learners is like driving with the emergency brake on.

Peter Vaill labels the traditional learning paradigm as *institutional*. It assumes that the goal can be specified in advance; that the learner can be motivated to adopt this goal; that the learner will adapt to the institution's pace; and that learning is a matter of getting the right answers. Vaill argues that this kind of system is better for indoctrination and control than for learning, and that it often increases meaninglessness instead of creating meaning.

In contrast, he proposes "learning as a way of being" as a foundation for learning organizations. In this paradigm, learning has at least seven characteristics:

1. It is self-directed (learners not only pace themselves, they decide what and how to learn).
2. It is creative (it emphasizes exploration rather than assimilation of prepackaged knowledge).
3. It is expressive (learners learn by doing).
4. It is feeling (learners are conscious of their emotional, states and use them as markers and clues in the learning process).
5. It is on-line (learners situate their learning in the real-world, with all the complexity and vividness that implies).
6. It is continual (learners move from one issue to another, unconcerned about timetables and boundaries).

7. It is reflexive (learners are conscious of and reflective about their learning activities).

Vaill reports that whenever he asks leaders to describe something they're good at and how they learned it, these elements are almost always present, whereas hardly anyone attributes important knowledge to institutional learning. (However, he notes that institutional training can be a productive element in meaningful learning, as long as the learner has consciously chosen it to accomplish certain goals.)

This new view of learning has several implications for principals wishing to accelerate the learning curve in their school. Most obviously, the key decisions about learning must be made by teachers themselves. The traditional pattern in which an administrator (or even an inservice council) selects topics for mass training sessions undercuts the learning process before it gets started.

Second, the school must provide (or promote) diversity of learning experiences, ranging from action research to peer coaching to networking. Not everyone learns in the same way or at the same pace or has the same needs. Just as many schools have discovered the importance of appealing to different student learning styles, teachers benefit from the same diversity.

Finally, opportunities should be provided for reflection on what is being learned and making decisions about what needs to be learned. Senge says that even the most intriguing new ideas won't take root unless they are accompanied by some kind of learning process.

> A learning process is a process that occurs over time whereby people's beliefs, ways of seeing the world, and ultimately their skills and capabilities change.... Learning occurs "at home," so to speak, in the sense that it must be integrated into our lives, and it always takes time and effort. (O'Neil)

PROFESSIONAL COMMUNITY

In the best schools, learning seems to become part of the culture, sinking its roots into everything that teachers and principals do. Sharon Kruse and Karen Seashore Louis have suggested that a strong foundation can be provided by developing what they call "professional community." Schools with a strong sense of professional community exhibit collective responsibility for results, decisions based on professional values rather than bureaucratic rules, and flexible roles that cross traditional boundaries.

Kruse and Seashore Louis suggest that professional communities are built on five major components.

1. *Reflective dialogue.* Members of a professional community engage in continual conversation about their individual and collective efforts to accomplish the common mission.

2. *Deprivatization of practice.* Professional community makes teaching public. Rather than closing the classroom door behind them, teachers invite colleagues in as observers, partners, or coaches. This public sharing not only expands the perspectives of teachers, it reinforces the values that bind them together.

3. *Collective focus on student learning.* In a professional community, teachers are more concerned with student learning than with teaching methods. They feel responsible for outcomes, not just input.

4. *Collaboration.* Members of a professional community work together at a deep level, doing more than sharing lesson plans or discussing students. Their collaboration is based on respect for others' expertise, and they use each other as consultants on teaching and learning.

5. *Shared norms and values.* Professional communities are based on the moral authority that comes from a common belief system. They tend to share a basic agreement over the purpose of the school, the nature of children, and the roles of teachers, administrators, and parents.

As with vision, professional community is enhanced through a combination of structural and cultural supports. Community is more likely to develop when teachers have time to meet and talk; have common spaces in which to meet; are given formal opportunities to work together; have well-developed communication structures (for example, e-mail and regular faculty meetings); and have been given considerable decision-making autonomy.

In addition, Kruse and Seashore Louis have found that community is enhanced by supportive leaders, openness to improvement, mutual trust, strong socialization processes for newcomers to the community, and a commitment to expertise and effectiveness in teaching.

FOCUSED LEARNING

With this emphasis on "learning as a way of being" and "professional community," it would be easy to romanticize the learning organization as a place of enthusiastic learning, zestful creativity, and spirited professional dialogue. Those elements are there, but the organizational-change literature also hints that the most effective learning is highly disciplined. That is, it never strays too far from the core practices that determine success or failure.

When Elmore and colleagues examined restructuring in a number of schools, they found that perceived reforms often didn't go beyond a surface gloss. Even when there was a guiding vision that was accepted by teachers, closer examination revealed that the new methods weren't significantly different from the old ones. Teachers believed themselves to be using a new philosophy, but their teaching showed inconsistent application of the new ideas.

Elmore's team attributed this inconsistency to lack of opportunity for critical reflection with other teachers, combined with a professional norm of not challenging others' teaching. Thus teachers had little basis for evaluating the success of their new methods. In schools that had a reflective and collaborative culture, teaching practices were more consistent with the espoused philosophy.

Elmore and his colleagues concluded that significant change in core practices resulted from focused teacher learning. "Deep, systematic knowledge of practice—in both abstract and concrete terms—is what distinguishes teachers who do ambitious teaching from those who are struggling to do it."

Interestingly, a similar lesson comes from the U.S. Army, which in the last two decades has aimed at becoming a learning organization (Gordon Sullivan and Michael Harper). One key tool is the "After Action Review" (AAR) in which a facilitator helps participants dissect, examine, and assess the results of a training exercise. The discussion in an AAR is concrete, detailed, and technical, but it boils down to three questions:

- What happened?
- Why did it happen?
- What should we do about it?

The AAR assumes that there is a common standard for success (that is, everyone agrees on what should have happened); if not, the discussion will reveal the discrepancy. It is not a critique in which leaders pass judgment on subordinates, but a team exercise devoted to improving everyone's performance (indeed, commanders are often chagrined to find that the orders they issued so crisply turned out to be ambiguous). Sullivan and Harper concede that the AAR is difficult, time-consuming, and sometimes painful, but that "the return on investment, measured by improved performance, is very high."

Whatever means is used (peer coaching is one possibility), leaders must work to keep the learning focused on the things that count most.

THE LEADER'S ROLE·

Because the learning organization concept is so new, and so little studied, the role of the leader has not been completely spelled out. But given the characteristics of a learning organization, we can speculate that several roles will be critical.

First and foremost, the leader of a learning organization is guardian of the vision that both inspires teacher learning and keeps it focused. Guardianship does not imply mindless adherence to the original statement; the learning that the vision stimulates will almost always lead to refinements and modifications. Rather, it requires the principal to be fully engaged with the vision at all times. Senge says:

> For anybody really serious in this work, you'll spend 20 to 40 percent of your time—forever—continually working on getting people to reflect on and articulate what it is they're really trying to create. It's never ending. (O'Neil)

Second, the principal is the school's preeminent learner, modeling the essential qualities of an effective lifelong learner. This means not only going to conferences, taking courses, and reading journals, but visibly demonstrating a passion for vision-driven learning. In particular, the principal must show:

- a gift for asking the kind of open-ended questions that mark the beginning of all meaningful learning: What's happening here? Is it what we want? What would happen if...?

- a willingness to follow abstract questions with concrete actions that will generate some answers

- the insight and integrity to admit that new knowledge has undermined a deeply held conviction or a pet idea

This last quality is especially important because of the human capacity for denial. Chris Argyris, after studying the learning processes of management consultants—generally a bright, perceptive group—was surprised at how easily their own failures led to defensiveness and finger-pointing rather than to new insights into their own behavior.

The same tendency can often be found in teachers, who see themselves (accurately) as dedicated and hard-working and who can only explain their failures by putting the blame elsewhere. As one teacher put it, "Schools aren't broken. Society is broken" (Farkas and Johnson). The problem with such responses, says Argyris, is not that they are wrong—often they are quite perceptive—but that they stop learning cold. If the problem lies elsewhere, then we don't need to look any farther for solutions.

Finally, the principal is a learning facilitator, making sure that resources flow where they are needed, that promising ideas are connected with the right people, and that teachers get personal support and encouragement in pursuing their learning agendas. White and colleagues note that simple fixes are rare in today's environment. There are many good ideas, but

> they have to be applied at the right time, in the right circumstances by the right people with the right intentions. They have to be adapted, molded, sometimes cajoled into the reality of the situation. And then they must be refined, developed, enhanced, perhaps replaced.

No one, not even the most brilliant or charismatic leader, can design, control, or order all the learning needed. But any principal can remove some of the barriers and provide incentives for others to take charge of their own learning.

FINAL THOUGHTS

Like vision, the learning organization is a noble concept that is much easier to talk about than to create, and there are still far too many things we don't know about it. As they survey their inbaskets, filled with items tagged "Urgent!", principals would surely be excused for putting the idea on the back burner.

Yet it would be harder to excuse a principal who simply wrote off the idea as a utopian fantasy. For one thing, schools with those characteristics do exist; imperfect as they are, they serve as a reminder of what schools can be. More importantly, as Sullivan and Harper note, the learning organization is less a destination than a direction, less a matter of "being" than "becoming." Any school can begin the process from any point, taking small steps or large ones. In the words of Robert Fritz:

> Greatness is not a utopian ideal demanding conformity to a set of prescribed values, goals, or codes for behavior. Rather, it is an organization that continually takes a stand for its values and dreams; an organization in which the highest in the human spirit can be expressed; an organization that continually reaches out toward its future. It is certainly not perfect, but in its imperfection lies the seeds of its learning. It is alive, dynamic, and growing, and when we are in its presence, we immediately recognize its heights and depths, for it seems to evoke within us a call to be our best and most noble. Who wouldn't want to work in an organization like that?

CONCLUSION

As I noted in the introduction to this book, the study of vision does not yet benefit from (and perhaps never will) the kind of rigorous empirical studies that lead inexorably to firm prescriptions. Like much of school leadership, vision appears to be a product of thoughtful craftsmanship rather than the application of universal rules.

Even so, some generalizations seem warranted:

1. *Developing organizational vision is an act of leadership, not a technical skill.* It requires a strong sense of moral purpose, a deep knowledge of people, and unwavering persistence.

2. *Visions are not created whole; rather, they evolve over time.* Vision is often equated with revelation: it comes in the middle of the night to a brilliant leader, who transmits it, fully formed, to his or her followers and then inspires them to carry it out. The reality seems far more complex:. In most of the accounts we have, visions become real only as they are lived out, with continual experimentation and adaptation.

3. *There is no universal pathway to vision.* Some schools develop a workable vision through a formal, self-conscious process. Others follow a more serendipitous path, taking dozens of small actions that gradually grow into something larger. What works best can only be determined through careful analysis and reflection by those on the scene. As much as we might wish otherwise, vision is never a paint-by-numbers exercise.

4. *Leading with vision is not a mystical act.* So-called "visionary" leaders do not have a direct pipeline to the future; they are not necessarily charismatic or spellbinding speakers; and, whatever their public facade, they suffer from doubt and uncertainty about as much as the average person. Most would probably fit comfortably into William Bridges's speculations about human achievement:

> Most of what has been worth doing since the beginning of time has been accomplished by people who were (like you and me, most of the time) tired, self-doubting, ambivalent, and more than a little discouraged. (1994)

In short, visionary leadership comes from rather ordinary people who are able to remember why they are there and who persist in trying to do something about it.

If there is anything that sets them aside from others, it may be courage—the courage to admit that we are not currently fulfilling our ideals, and that regardless of risks we must reach beyond the comfortable status quo.

True visions—the kind that make the inner self shout, "Yes!"— are scary. In part, we fear failure, worrying about criticism if we publicly announce an ambitious goal and then fail to achieve it. (Or perhaps we fear the sense of disillusionment that comes from realizing the gap between fond dreams and harsh reality.) Failure is certainly a possibility; the odds are indeed formidable, and no one is guaranteed success. But the alternative to trying (and *perhaps* failing) is neatly summed up by hockey great Wayne Gretzky: "You miss one hundred percent of the shots you don't take" (Warren Bennis and Burt Nanus).

Oddly enough, in the complex landscape of human emotions, we may also fear *success*, feeling ourselves somehow unworthy of the task. Nelson Mandela addressed that issue in his inaugural address, as he shared his vision for South Africa:

> We ask ourselves, who am I to be brilliant, gorgeous, talented, and fabulous? Actually, who are you not to be?...We are born to make manifest the Glory of God that is within us. It's not just in some of us, it's in everyone, and as we let our own light shine, we consciously give other people permission to do the same. As we are liberated from our own fear, our presence automatically liberates others. (Ken Blanchard and Terry Waghorn)

If you need a source of courage, just walk through the corridors of your school, listening, watching, and tuning in to the human potential all around you: hundreds of small lights, passionately wanting to shine. And waiting for a leader.

SAMPLE MISSION AND VISION STATEMENTS

The following mission and vision statements have been adopted by the Bartholomew Consolidated School Corporation in Columbus, Indiana.

According to Dr. Linda DeClue, assistant superintendent for curriculum and instruction, the statements were initiated in 1995 at a two-day retreat of the district's administrators (central office, building principals, and program heads). With the help of an outside facilitator, participants considered questions such as "What does an ideal elementary school look like?"

The themes developed at the retreat were used by a core planning group to draft a preliminary statement, which was then reviewed by all participants and revised accordingly. The revised documents were then reviewed by the school board and modified again. After one more review by the entire group, the statements were communicated throughout the school community.

The district plans to use the statements as a guide when schools prepare for their state performance-based-accreditation process. They will also provide a framework as individual schools develop or revise their own visions. While the statements are too recent to gauge long-term effects, DeClue says that they have become part of the daily conversation in the district, with staff members asking, "How does this fit with the mission and vision?"

MISSION

Bartholomew Consolidated School Corporation's mission is to

create a process that achieves educational excellence for all through a commitment to:

- Individual Student Success
- Professional Growth and Development
- Accountability
- Continuous Improvement

The end result of educational excellence is the mastery of skills, the acquisition of knowledge, and the ability to use technology so all learners become productive, responsible citizens, who lead meaningful, challenging lives.

VISION

THE CORE:

Students in the Bartholomew Consolidated School Corporation will receive an education designed to meet their *individual needs*. This includes:

- flexible time schedules (minutes, hours, days and years)
- individual learning plans with individual goals for each student
- self-directed and self-paced learning that does not sort students according to age, grade, or ability
- multiple program choices
- education in becoming a responsible, respectful and productive citizen
- student-parent-teacher input into the process of learning

IMMEDIATE SUPPORT:

Students are *supported* in their educational efforts in a variety of ways:

- strong home/school connection
- partnerships with businesses/community/mentors
- comprehensive services for students available as needed (counseling, special education, medical, nutritional, social service agencies, child care before and after school)
- safe, nonthreatening supportive environment that is inclusive and where diversity is accepted and welcomed

- facilities that have a variety of technologies; multiple options for instruction; accessible to all; necessary resources; viewed as community centers

TEACHER/PARENT COMMUNITY SUPPORT:

In order to achieve this vision for students, adults involved in the educational process will view their roles in new and expanded ways:

- parents as partners
- teachers/parents/community members as facilitators/mentors for students
- teachers collaborating/cooperating with one another; planning together; time to reflect and plan
- teachers participating in continuous growth opportunities
- all adults (bus drivers, cafeteria staff, custodians, teachers, teacher assistants, parents, community members) are involved in planning, decision making, continuously improving system
- all adults in school have students' success as their focus—not programs or facilities
- continuously seek ways to improve system—decisions based on data
- all adults in school are responsible and creative in their use of resources (money, technology, people, facilities)

ACCOUNTABILITY:

Student progress is *assessed* continuously in a variety of ways, including:

- collections of student products (art work, projects, writing samples, other examples of student work, examples of problem-solving)
- tests, quizzes
- standardized tests
- participastion/involvement/cooperation/effort
- self-assessment (student selection of best efforts, goals set and met)
- comparison to previous work efforts
- frequent reports to parents (conferencing with parents, teachers, students)
- the ability to solve problems using multiple strategies

BIBLIOGRAPHY

Many of the items in this bibliography are indexed in ERIC's monthly catalog *Resources in Education* (*RIE*). Reports in *RIE* are indicated by an "ED" number. Journal articles, indexed in ERIC's companion catalog, *Current Index to Journals in Education,* are indicated by an "EJ" number.

Most items with an ED number are available from ERIC Document Reproduction Service (EDRS), 7420 Fullerton Rd., Suite 110, Springfield, VA 22153-2852.

To order from EDRS, specify the ED number, type of reproduction desired—microfiche (MF) or paper copy (PC), and number of copies. Add postage to the cost of all orders and include check or money order payable to EDRS. For credit card orders, call 1-800-443-3742.

Ackerman, Richard H.; Gordon A. Donaldson, Jr.; and Rebecca van der Bogert. *Making Sense As a School Leader: Persisting Questions, Creative Opportunities.* San Francisco: Jossey-Bass, 1996. 186 pages. ED 390 157.

Amsler, Mary, and Kayla Kirsch. *Diagnostic Tools for the Systemic Reform of Schools.* San Francisco: Far West Lab for Educational Research and Development, 1994. 91 pages. ED 371 460.

Argyris, Chris. *On Organizational Learning.* Cambridge, Massachusetts: Blackwell, 1993. 450 pages.

Barth, Roland S. *Improving Schools from Within: Teachers, Parents, and Principals Can Make the Difference.* San Francisco: Jossey-Bass, 1990. 190 pages. ED 319 126.

Bennis, Warren, and Burt Nanus. *Leaders: Strategies for Taking Charge.* Second edition. New York: HarperCollins, 1997.

Bennis, Warren; Jagdish Parikh; and Ronnie Lessem. *Beyond Leadership: Balancing Economics, Ethics, and Ecology.* Cambridge, Massachusetts: Blackwell Publishers, 1994.

Blanchard, Ken, and Terry Waghorn. *Mission Possible: Becoming a World-Class Organization While There's Still Time.* New York: McGraw-Hill, 1997. 226 pages.

Blase, Jo, and Joseph Blase. *The Fire Is Back! Principals Sharing School Governance.* Thousand Oaks, California: Corwin Press, 1997. 166 pages.

Blase, Joseph, and Jo Roberts Blase. *Empowering Teachers: What Successful Principals Do.* Thousand Oaks, California: Corwin Press, 1994. 192 pages. ED 377 576.

Blase, Joseph; Jo Blase; Gary L. Anderson; and Sherry Dungan. *Democratic Principals in Action: Eight Pioneers.* Thousand Oaks, California: Corwin Press, 1995. 193 pages. ED 380 890.

Blumberg, Arthur. *School Administration As a Craft: Foundations of Practice.* Boston: Allyn and Bacon, 1989. 238 pages. ED 304 773.

Blumberg, Arthur, and William Greenfield. *The Effective Principal: Perspectives on School Leadership.* Second Edition. Boston: Allyn and Bacon, 1986. 253 pages. ED 283 274.

Bolman, Lee G., and Terrence E. Deal. *Reframing Organizations: Artistry, Choice, and Leadership.* San Francisco: Jossey-Bass, 1991. 492 pages. ED 371 457.

Boyd, Victoria, and Shirley M. Hord. "Principals and the New Paradigm: Schools as Learning Communities." Paper presented at the annual meeting of the American Educational Research Association, 1994. 33 pages. ED 373 428.

Bradley, Ann. "What Price Success?" *Education Week*, November 22, 1995.

Bridges, William. *Managing Transitions: Making the Most of Change.* Reading, Massachusetts: Addison-Wesley, 1991. 130 pages.

_____. *JobShift: How to Prosper in a Workplace without Jobs.* Reading, Massachusetts: Addison-Wesley, 1994.

Burkan, Wayne. *Wide-Angle Vision: Beat Your Competition by Focusing on Fring Competitors, Lost Customers, and Rogue Employees.* New York: John Wiley, 1996. 75 pages.

Chenoweth, Thomas, and James Kushman. "Courtship and School Restructuring: Building Early Commitment to School Change for At-Risk Students." Paper presented at the annual meeting of the American Educational Research Association, Atlanta, April 1993. 56 pages. ED 360 715.

Cohen, Margaret W., and Loyal Packer. *When the Keeper of the Vision Changes: Leadership in an Accerlerated School.* Paper presented at the annaul meeting of the American Educational Research Association, New Orleans, Louisiana, April 1994. 20 pages. ED 373 429.

Collins, James C., and Jerry I. Porras. *Built to Last: Successful Habits of Visionary Companies.* New York: HarperBusiness, 1994. 322 pages.

Conley, David T. *Are You Ready to Restructure? A Guidebook for Educators, Parents, and Community Members.* Thousand Oaks, California: Corwin Press, 1996. 181 pages. ED 390 179.

Conley, David T., Diane M. Dunlap, and Paul Goldman. "The 'Vision Thing' and School Restructuring." *OSSC Report* 32, 2 (Winter 1992): 1-8. Eugene, Oregon: Oregon School Study Council. ED 343 246.

Conley, David T., and Paul Goldman. *Facilitative Leadership: How Principals Lead Without Dominating.* OSSC Bulletin Series. Eugene, Oregon: Oregon School Study Council, August 1994. 52 pages. ED 379 728.

Conway, James A., and Frank Calzi. "The Dark Side of Shared Decision Making." *Educational Leadership* 53, 4 (December 1995/January 1996): 45-49. EJ 517 892.

Covey, Stephen R.; A. Roger Merrill; and Rebecca Merrill. *First Things First: To Live, To Love, To Learn, To Leave a Legacy.* New York: Simon and Schuster, 1994. 360 pages.

Csikszentmihalyi, Mihaly. *Creativity.* New York: Harper Collins, 1996.

Cuban, Larry. *How Teachers Taught: Constancy and Change in the American Classroom, 1890-1980.* New York: Longman, 1984. 306 pages. ED 383 498.

Cunningham, William G., and Donn W. Gresso. *Cultural Leadership: The Culture of Excellence in Education.* Boston: Allyn and Bacon, 1993. 285 pages. ED 377 582.

Davis, Stan, and Jim Botkin. *The Monster Under the Bed: How Business Is Mastering the Opportunity of Knowledge for Profit.* New York: Simon and Schuster, 1994.

Deal, Terrence E. "Symbols and Symbolic Activity." In *Images of Schools: Structures and Roles in Organizational Behavior,* edited by Samuel Bacharach and Bryan Mundell. Thousand Oaks, California: Corwin Press, 1995. 425 pages. ED 383 089.

Deal, Terrence E., and Kent D. Peterson. *The Leadership Paradox: Balancing Logic and Artistry in Schools.* San Francisco: Jossey-Bass, 1994. 133 pages. ED 371 455.

Dewey, John. *The Public and Its Problems.* Denver: Alan Swallow, 1927.

Dolan, W. Patrick. *Restructuring Our Schools: A Primer on Systems Change,* edited by Lilot Moorman. Kansas City, Kansas: Systems and Organization, 1994.

Drucker, Peter F. "The Age of Social Transformation." *Atlantic Monthly* 274, 5 (November 1994): 53-80.

——————. *Innovation and Entrepreneurship: Practice and Principles.* New York: Harper & Row, 1985.

Elmore, Richard F.; Penelope L. Peterson; and Sarah J. McCarthey. *Restructuring in the Classroom: Teaching, Learning, and School Organization.* San Francisco: Jossey-Bass, 1996. 257 pages.

Farkas, Steve, and Jean Johnson. *Given the Circumstances: Teachers Talk About Public Education Today.* New York: Public Agenda, 1996.

Fredonia (New York) *Censor and Union.* July 10, 1872.

Fritz, Robert. *Corporate Tides: The Inescapable Laws of Organizational Structure.* San Francisco: Berrett-Koehler, 1996.

Fullan, Michael G., and Matthew B. Miles. "Getting Reform Right: What Works and What Doesn't." *Phi Delta Kappan* 73, 10 (June 1992): 744-52. EJ 445 727.

Fullan, Michael G.; with Suzanne Stiegelbauer. *The New Meaning of Educational Change.* Second edition. New York: Teachers College Press, 1991. 401 pages. ED 354 588.

Gardner, Howard in collaboration with Emma Laskin. *Leading Minds: An Anatomy of Leadership.* New York: Basic Books, 1995. 400 pages.

Gastil, John. *Democracy in Small Groups: Participation, Decision Making, and Communication.* Philadelphia, Pennsylvania: New Society Publishers, 1993. 213 pages.

Gideonse, Hendrik. "Organizing Schools to Encourage Teacher Inquiry." In *Restructuring Schools: The Next Generation of Educational Reform,* edited by Richard F. Elmore and Associates. 97-124. San Francisco: Jossey-Bass, 1990. ED 356 519.

Gitlin, Andrew, and Frank Margonis. "The Political Aspect of Reform: Teacher Resistance as Good Sense." *American Journal of Education* 103, 4 (August 1995): 377-405. EJ 515 546.

Greenfield, William D., Jr. "The Micropolitics of Leadership in an Urban Elementary School." In *The Politics of Life in Schools: Power, Conflict, and Cooperation,* edited by Joseph Blase. Newbury Park, California: Sage Publications, 1991. 271 pages. ED 336 834.

Griffin, Gary A. "Influences of Shared Decision Making on School and Classroom Activity: Conversations with Five Teachers." *The Elementary School Journal* 96, 1 (September 1995): 29-45. EJ 510 577.

Grove, Andrew S. *Only the Paranoid Survive: How to Exploit the Crisis Points That Challenge Every Company and Career.* New York: Currency Doubleday: 1996.

Hammer, Michael, and Steven A. Stanton. *The Reengineering Revolution: A Handbook.* New York: Harper Collins Publishers, 1995. 336 pages.

Haynes, Mary. Unpublished paper. Aberdeen, Washington, 1996.

Hong, Laraine K. *Surviving School Reform: A Year in the Life of One School.* New York: Teachers College Press, 1996. 196 pages.

Hoyle, John R. *Leadership and Futuring: Making Visions Happen.* Thousand Oaks, California: Corwin Press, 1995. 83 pages. ED 386 809.

Hurst, David K. *Crisis and Renewal: Meeting the Challenge of Organizational Change.* Boston: Harvard Business School Press, 1995.

Isaacson, Nancy, and Jerry Bamburg. "Can Schools Become Learning Organizations?" *Educational Leadership* 50, 3 (November 1992): 42-44. EJ 454 329.

Johnson, James H. *Student Voice: Motivating Students Through Empowerment.* OSSC Bulletin Series. Eugene, Oregon: Oregon School Study Council, October 1991. ED 337 875.

Johnson, Jean, and John Immerwahr. "First Things First: What Americans Expect from the Public Schools." *American Educator* 18, 4 (Winter 1994) 4-6, 8, 11-13, 44-45. EJ 498 493.

Johnson, Marlene. *Redefining Leadership: A Case Study of Hollibrook Elementary School. Project Report.* Urbana, Illinois: National Center for School Leadership, 1992. 79 pages. ED 360 687.

Johnson, Susan Moore. Redesigning Teachers' Work." In *Restructuring Schools: The Next Generation of Educational Reform,* edited by Richard F. Elmore and others. 125-151. San Francisco: Jossey-Bass, 1990a. 329 pages. ED 356 519.

_____. *Teachers at Work: Achieving Success in Our Schools.* New York: Basic Books, 1990b. 395 pages. ED 336 387.

Kaufman, Roger. *Mapping Educational Success: Strategic Thinking and Planning for School Administrators.* Thousand Oaks, California: Corwin Press, 1995.

Kerka, Sandra. *The Learning Organization. Myths and Realities.* Columbus, Ohio: ERIC Clearinghouse on Adult, Career, and Vocational Educational Education. 4 pages. ED 388 802.

Keyser, Thomas. *Mining Group Gold.* Chicago: Irwin, 1995.

Kotter, John P. *Leading Change.* Bostons: Harvard Business Review Press, 1996. 187 pages.

Kouzes, James M., and Barry Z. Posner. *The Leadership Challenge: How To Keep Getting Extraordinary Things Done in Organizations.* San Francisco: Jossey-Bass, 1995. 405 pages.

Kruse, Sharon D., and Karen Seashore Louis. "An Emerging Framework for Analyzing School-Based Professional Community." Paper presented at the annual meeting of the American Educational Research Association, Atlanta Georgia, April 1993. 31 pages. ED 358 537.

Leithwood, Kenneth, and Robert Aitken. *Making Schools Smarter: A System for Monitoring School and District Progress.* Thousand Oaks, California: Corwin Press, 1995. 206 pages. ED 386 824.

Leithwood, Kenneth; Paul T. Begley; and J. Bradley Cousins. *Developing Expert Leadership for Future Schools.* London: The Falmer Press, 1994. 331 pages. ED 394 172.

Leithwood, Kenneth; Doris Jantzi; and Rosanne Steinbach. "An Organizational Learning Perspective on School Responses to Central Policy Initiatives." Paper presented at the annual meeting of the American Educational Research Association, San Francisco, April 1995. 38 pages. ED 385 932.

Liontos, Lynn Balster. *Transformational Leadership: Profile of a High School Principal.* OSSC Bulletin Series. Eugene, Oregon: Oregon School Study Council, October 1993. 50 pages. ED 363 969.

Liontos, Lynn Balster, and Larry Lashway. "Shared Decision-Making." In *School Leadership: Handbook for Excellence,* third edition, edited by Philip Piele and Stuart Smith. 226-50. Eugene, Oregon: ERIC Clearinghouse on Educational Management, 1997.

Lonnquist, M. Peg, and Jean A. King. "Changing the Tire on a Moving Bus: Barriers To the Development of Community in a New Teacher-Led School." Paper presented at the annual meeting of the American Educational Research Association, Atlanta, Georgia, December 1993. 31 pages. ED 366 064.

Louis, Karen Seashore, and Matthew B. Miles. *Improving the Urban High School: What Works and Why.* New York: Teachers College Press, 1990. 357 pages. ED 327 623.

Mathews, David. *Is There a Public for Public Schools?* Dayton, Ohio: Kettering Foundation Press, 1996. 81 pages. ED 400 600.

McDonald, Joseph P. "Steps in Planning Backwards: Early Lessons from the Schools." On-line paper. Coalition of Essential Schools, February 1992.

Manning, George; Kent Curtis; and Steve McMillan. *Building Community: The Human Side of Work.* Cincinnati: Thomson Executive Press. 1996.

Mintzberg, Henry. *The Rise and Fall of Strategic Planning: Reconceiving Roles for Planning, Plans, Planners.* New York: The Free Press, 1994. 458 pages.

Nanus, Burt. *Visionary Leadership: Creating a Compelling Sense of Direction for Your Organization.* San Francisco: Jossey-Bass, 1992. 237 pages. ED 350 948.

O'Neil, John. "On Schools As Learning Organizations: A Conversation With Peter Senge." *Educational Leadership* 52, 7 (April 1995): 20-23. EJ 502 905.

Rose, Michael. *Possible Lives: The Promise of Public Education in America.* Boston: Houghton Mifflin, 1995.

Sarason, Seymour. *Parental Involvement and the Political Principle: Why the Existing Governance Structure of Schools Should Be Abolished.* San Francisco: Jossey-Bass, 1995. 180 pages. ED 383 074.

Sashkin, Marshall. "The Visionary Principal: School Leadership for the Next Century." In *Educational Leadership and School Culture,* edited by Marshall Sashkin and Herbert Walberg. Berkeley, California: McCutchan Publishing Corporation, 1993. 195 pages. ED 367 056.

Schwartz, Peter. *The Art of the Long View.* New York: Doubleday, 1991. 258 pages.

Senge, Peter M. *The Fifth Discipline: The Art and Practice of the Learning Organization.* New York: Doubleday, 1990. 424 pages.

Senge, Peter M., Art Kleiner; Charlotte Roberts; Richard B. Ross; and Bryan J. Smith. *The Fifth Discipline Fieldbook: Strategies and Tools for Building a Learning Organization.* New York: Doubleday, 1994.

Sergiovanni, Thomas J. *Moral Leadership: Getting to the Heart of School Improvement.* San Francisco: Jossey-Bass, 1992. 173 pages. ED 364 965.

Serow, Robert C.; Deborah J. Eaker; and Krista D. Forrest. " 'I Want to See Some Kind of Growth Out of Them': What the Service Ethic Means to Teacher-Education Students." *American Educational Research Journal* 31, 1 (Spring 1994): 27-48. EJ 482 574.

Shedd, Joseph B., and Samuel Bacharach. *Tangled Hierarchies: Teachers as Professionals and the Management of Schools.* San Francisco: Jossey-Bass, 1991. 232 pages. ED 354 586.

Sheive, Linda Tinelli, and Marian Beauchamp Schoenheit. "Vision and the Work Life of Educational Leaders." In *Leadership: Examining the Elusive,* edited by Linda Scheive and Marian Schoenheit. Alexandria, Virginia: Association for Supervision and Curriculum Development, 1987. 144 pages. ED 278 154.

Starratt, Robert J. *Leaders With Vision: The Quest for School Renewal.* Thousand Oaks, California: Corwin Press, 1995. 144 pages. ED 389 074.

Strebel, Paul. "Why Do Employees Resist Change?" *Harvard Business Review* (May-June 1996): 86-92.

Sullivan, Gordon R., and Michael V. Harper. *Hope Is Not a Method: What Business Leaders Can Learn from America's Army.* New York: Times Business, 1996.

Tewel, Kenneth J. *New Schools for a New Century: A Leader's Guide to High School Reform.* Delray Beach, Florida: St. Lucie Press, 1995. 231 pages. ED 386 797.

Vaill, Peter B. *Learning As a Way of Being: Strategies for Survival in a World of Permanent White Water.* San Francisco: Jossey-Bass, 1996. 218 pages.

Wagner, Tony. "Building a Shared Vision:,Structured Dialogues About Important Questions." *New Schools, New Communities* 11, 3 (Spring 1995): 19-26. EJ 505 954.

Weiss, Carol H. "The Four 'I's' of School Reform: How Interests, Ideology, Information, and Institution Affect Teachers and Principals." *Harvard Educational Review* 65, 4 (Winter 1995): 571-92. EJ 514 341.

Wheatley, Margaret J. *Leadership and the New Science: Learning about Organization from an Orderly Universe.* San Francisco: Berrett-Koehler, 1994. 166 pages. ED 390 177.

White, Randall P.; Philip Hodgson; and Stuart Crainer. *The Future of Leadership: Riding the Corporate Rapids into the 21st Century.* London: Pitman Publishing, 1996.

Wincek, Jean. *Negotiating the Maze of School Reform: How Metaphor Shapes Culture in a New Magnet School.* New York: Teachers College Press, 1995. 160 pages. ED 391 253.

Yankelovich, Daniel. *Coming To Public Judgment: Making Democracy Work in a Complex World.* Syracuse, New York: Syracuse University Press, 1991. 290 pages.

OTHER TITLES

School Leadership:
Handbook for Excellence
Edited by Stuart C. Smith and Philip K. Piele • Third
Edition • 1997 • xvi + 432 pages • Cloth ISBN 0-86552-
134-4 ($29.95) **Code: EMOSLC.** Paper ISBN 0-86552-
135-2 ($19.95) **Code: EMOSLP.**

Five new chapters—on ethics, vision, school culture,
quality work teams, and shared decision-making—appear in this latest
edition of the Clearinghouse's flagship title. The handbook suggests
the knowledge, values, structure, and skills necessary for a leader to
inspire all members of the school community to work together toward
the goal of educational excellence.

Each chapter is a simple yet detailed exposition of ideas and
evidence on the topic, free of jargon and technical data. Sections also
spell out implications, recommendations, or guidelines for putting
knowledge into practice.

Learning Experiences in School Renewal:
An Exploration of Five Successful Programs
Edited by Bruce Joyce and Emily Calhoun • 1996 • 6
x 9 inches • viii + 208 pages • perfect bind • ISBN: 0-
86552-133-6 • $14.50. **Code: EMOLES.**

This book provides candid, captivating accounts of
the experiences of five school districts that sought to
build learning communities for adults and children alike.

The five programs share three characteristics: a primary focus
on improving student learning; an investment in people as a major
school-improvement strategy; and a goal of learning through the
process and thereby expanding understanding of school renewal and
staff development.

Making fascinating reading, the cases suggest that significant,
lasting improvement can be achieved relatively quickly when effective
models of teaching are coupled with well-designed, ongoing staff
development that transfers into real changes in curriculum and
instruction.

Transforming School Culture: Stories, Symbols, Values, and the Leader's Role

Stephen Stolp and Stuart C. Smith • 1995 • 6 x 9 inches • xii + 92 pages • perfect bind • ISBN: 0-86552-132-8 • $12.50. **Code: EMOTSC.**

What distinguishes an ineffective school culture from an effective one, and how can a school culture that fails to support excellence be changed? Stolp and Smith provide some answers.

This refreshing book demystifies the concept of *school culture.* The authors clarify the meaning of culture and offer many examples to illustrate its significance in schools. Their goal is to help school administrators and teachers cultivate a school culture that is "a positive force for excellence."

Roadmap to Restructuring: Charting the Course of Change in American Education

Second Edition • David T. Conley • 1997 • 6 x 9 inches • xvi+ 571 pages • Paper • ISBN 0-86552-137-9 • $23.95. **Code: EMORMP** • Cloth • ISBN 0-86552-136-0 • $34.95. **Code: EMORMC**

Roadmap to Restructuring has been a Clearinghouse best-seller ever since the first edition was published in 1993. Now it's been updated and expanded.

The new edition adds more than 100 pages of text plus subject and author indexes. Most of the new content was added to part 3, the Dimensions of Restructuring, where Conley sets forth a framework of twelve dimensions of restructuring. These dimensions sort out the multitude of projects taking place under the banner of restructuring.

Purchase order or prepayment required. (Sorry, we cannot take orders by phone.) Add 10% for S & H (minimum $4.00). Make payment to **University of Oregon/ ERIC** and mail to ERIC/CEM, 5207 University of Oregon, Eugene, Oregon 97403-5207. Shipping is by UPS ground or equivalent.

Telephone (800) 438-8841

Fax (541) 346-2334